T.1

Powers Within

POWERS WITHIN

Selections from the Works of

SRI AUROBINDO

and

THE MOTHER

Compiled with an Introduction by

A. S. Dalal

Sri Aurobindo Ashram
Pondicherry

First edition 1998
Fourth impression 2008

Rs 55
ISBN 978-81-7058-535-0

Published by Sri Aurobindo Ashram Publication Department,
Pondicherry 605 002
Web   http://www.sabda.in

Printed at Sri Aurobindo Ashram Press, Pondicherry
PRINTED IN INDIA

From Sri Aurobindo's *Savitri*

In hands sustained by a transfiguring Might
He caught up lightly like a giant's bow
Left slumbering in a sealed and secret cave
The powers that sleep unused in man within.

Book One — Canto Three, p. 26

In a body obscuring the immortal Spirit
A nameless Resident vesting unseen powers
With Matter's shapes and motives beyond thought
And the hazard of an unguessed consequence,
An omnipotent indiscernible Influence,
He sits, unfelt by the form in which he lives
And veils his knowledge by the groping mind.

Book One — Canto Four, p. 68

In our body's cells there sits a hidden Power
That sees the unseen and plans eternity,

Book Two — Canto Five, p. 169

There is a Power within that knows beyond
Our knowings;

Book Five — Canto Two, p. 397

A Seer, a strong Creator, is within,
The immaculate Grandeur broods upon your days,
Almighty powers are shut in Nature's cells.

Book Four — Canto Three, p. 370

CONTENTS

INTRODUCTION

The term "power" is often used to mean force of influence — political, financial or social. Such external power is to be distinguished from the powers within spoken of in this book, consisting of abilities, capacities or faculties which are inherent in the human constitution, though more or less dormant or undeveloped.

Powers of Consciousness

According to the Vedantic view, the fundamental reality constituting the human being as well as the universe is Chit or Consciousness. All energy, dynamism or power comes from consciousness, for, as Sri Aurobindo states, "Absolute consciousness is in its nature absolute power; the nature of Chit is Shakti [Force]."[1] Therefore, Chit is called also Chit-Shakti, Consciousness-Force. Thus the different forms of consciousness — physical, vital, mental, subliminal, subconscient and superconscient — are different formulations of powers of consciousness. In our ordinary state of consciousness we identify ourselves with our separate individual self called the ego, and seek power for the aggrandisement of the ego. But from a deeper point of view, all the endeavours of the ego are motivated unconsciously by the urge to discover one's true Self and its powers of consciousness.

---

[1] Sri Aurobindo, *The Life Divine*, Centenary Library Vol. 18, p. 570.

Latent Powers

Two types of latent powers may be distinguished. There are powers within us that are yet unevolved and for the most part unsuspected, if not disbelieved, such as clairvoyance, clairaudience, telepathy and other occult powers spoken of in the latter part of the book. There are other powers that we already possess and use but are latent in the sense of existing in quite a rudimentary and or undeveloped form. We do not regard these latter as "powers" because there seems to be nothing extraordinary about them. Such are the powers of thought, imagination, will, concentration, intuition and the like, which in their present state in most human beings are quite undeveloped in relation to what they could be at their highest potential. What we see in a genius is simply the flowering of powers which are either undeveloped or totally latent in us. As the Mother remarks, "There is a genius within everyone of us" (p. 6).

The possibility of developing one's potential to a remarkable degree exists also with physical powers and abilities pertaining to the body. An Olympic athlete has simply developed abilities which are present in some degree in everyone. The Mother gives examples (pp. 7-8) of how even our sensory abilities, such as sight and hearing, can be heightened to a miraculous degree, and remarks, "We can do infinitely more than we actually do" (p. 8).

Occult Powers

When people think of latent powers, especially in the East, they often think of occult powers mentioned a little earlier.

There are different attitudes both in the West and the East towards such powers. In the West, where such powers are generally called "psychic abilities", the majority of people look upon them with scepticism, attributing belief in them to credulity and gullibility. However, a growing number of Westerners do believe in the veracity of abilities claimed by the "psychics", such as the ability to obtain information through extrasensory perception, to affect objects and persons from a distance, to heal by invisible means and the like. Despite their erratic nature, such abilities have been sporadically employed in numerous fields, including medicine and dentistry, psychotherapy and counseling, police work, agriculture, archaeology and many others.

Psychiatrists tend to look upon persons who apparently possess psychic powers as abnormal, that is, suffering from a psychiatric disorder. Dr. Judith Orloff, a psychiatrist in Los Angeles and author of *Second Sight* (Thomas Moore, 1997) writes that she displayed paranormal abilities since the age of nine, but for years refrained from speaking about them because her mother and others around showed no understanding of these abilities and gave her the feeling she was abnormal. It was only when, after an out-of-body experience, she was seen at an institute for ESP that she learnt that she was gifted rather than psychiatrically ill. According to her estimate, perhaps based mainly on her own practice of psychiatry, about twenty-five percent of those who seek psychiatric help and are diagnosed as suffering from psychosis are in fact psychic rather than psychotic.

In the East, most people have tended to consider supernormal powers, or Siddhis (perfections) as they are called in India, to be marks of spiritual attainment. However, spiritual teachers of a high order have regarded occult powers as inferior and unrelated to spiritual attainment. One who seeks occult powers, remarked Ramakrishna, is like someone who being offered a boon by a king asks for a pumpkin. Some even hold that on the spiritual path one must desist not only from seeking occult powers but also from using them if one has acquired them. Regarding such an attitude, Sri Aurobindo writes:

"The idea that yogins do not or ought not to use these powers [having consciousness of things at a distance and intervening] I regard as an ascetic superstition. I believe that all yogins who have these powers do use them whenever they find that they are called from within to do so. They may refrain if they think the use in a particular case is contrary to the Divine Will or see that preventing one evil may be opening the door to a worse or for any other valid reason, but not from any general prohibitory rule. What is forbidden to everyone with a strong spiritual sense is to be a miracle-monger performing extraordinary things for show, for gain, for fame, out of vanity or pride."[2]

Occultism in Daily Life

Sri Aurobindo defines occultism as "the knowledge and right use of the hidden forces of Nature... — especially the forces of the subtle physical and supraphysical planes."[3] As the Mother points out (p. 17), in a way, everyone practises occultism without knowing it because everyone uses the powers of thought

---

[2] Sri Aurobindo, *Letters on Yoga*, Centenary Library Vol. 22, p. 481.
[3] Sri Aurobindo, *Letters on Yoga*, Centenary Library Vol. 22, p. 75.

and imagination which are in fact occult or hidden but which produce visible effects on oneself and others. The effects produced by our ordinary thought and imagination are meagre compared to what they could be if the powers were developed through training. In fact, most people are not even aware of the effects brought about by thought and imagination on our bodies and our external lives. Therefore these powers are often used in ways which are detrimental to us and others. An important step in developing the powers within us is to become more conscious of the powers we already possess and use as also of the effects they are producing in our daily lives, so that we may learn to use them more deliberately and beneficially.

Power from Within and Without

Power can be derived from external things or from our own being. For example, power for fighting illness can come from the use of external means such as medicines, or it can be summoned from within in the body's innate power of resistance. Until now, humanity in its efforts for gaining more and more power has endeavoured to obtain power in different areas predominantly from without through technological and scientific developments. Development of the powers within us has received far less attention, so that internal power has not only lagged far behind external power but has also deteriorated in some respects. Thus whereas great strides have been made in combating disease with the aid of external means, namely more powerful drugs and more advanced technology, there is an increasing prevalence of diseases related to the body's own immune system, such as cancer, arthritis, AIDS and others, indicating a deterioration of the body's own natural mechanisms of healing.

Apropos of the decrease in personal power that has resulted with the increase in technology, Joseph C. Pierce writes in his book, *The Bond of Power* (Dutton, 1981):

"We have long spoken of our technological devices as 'extensions' of our personal power.... In practice, though, every technological achievement really undermines, erodes, even replaces in one way or another, our ability it 'extends and enhances'."

As an example, Pierce states that whereas we have extended our powers of *aided* vision through technological devices such as the telescope and the microscope, our *own* visual power has deteriorated. Thus, in Texas, in 1900, about twelve percent of children at the age of eight had short-sightedness. In 1962, even at the age of six, approximately eighty percent of the children were found to have short-sightedness.

One of the signs of the dawning of the New Age — adumbrated by Sri Aurobindo and others — is that more and more people are seeking the development of powers within as evidenced by the emergence of the Human Potential Movement, training courses for the enhancement of sensory and paranormal abilities, devices for expansion of consciousness (trying to develop the inside from outside!) and the increasing popularity of meditation and other spiritual practices.

This book throws light on the nature of the various powers which we already possess and wield consciously or unconsciously, as well as latent powers within us which are as yet more or less undeveloped.

It should be noted that passages from the works of the Mother consist of talks given by her to the children of the Ashram, generally in answering questions put to her by the children.

Passages contained in the book have been selected so as to make the book of interest to the general reader as well as to the spiritual seeker.

A. S. Dalal

Powers Within

LATENT POWERS

An evolution of innate and latent but as yet unevolved powers of consciousness is not considered admissible by the modern mind, because these exceed our present formulation of Nature and, to our ignorant preconceptions founded on a limited experience, they seem to belong to the supernatural, to the miraculous and occult; for they surpass the known action of material Energy which is now ordinarily accepted as the sole cause and mode of things and the sole instrumentation of the World-Force. A human working of marvels, by the conscious being discovering and developing an instrumentation of material forces overpassing anything that Nature has herself organised, is accepted as a natural fact and an almost unlimited prospect of our existence; an awakening, a discovery, an instrumentation of powers of consciousness and of spiritual, mental and life forces overpassing anything that Nature or man has yet organised is not admitted as possible. But there would be nothing supernatural or miraculous in such an evolution, except in so far as it would be a super-nature or superior nature to ours just as human nature is a supernature or superior nature to that of animal or plant or material objects. Our mind and its powers, our use of reason, our mental intuition and insight, speech, possibilities of philosophical, scientific, aesthetic discovery of the truths and potencies of being and a control of its forces are an evolution that has taken place: yet it would seem impossible if we took our stand on the limited animal consciousness and its capacities; for there is nothing there to warrant so prodigious a progression. But still there are vague initial manifestations, rudimentary elements or arrested possibilities in the animal to which our reason and intelligence with their extraordinary developments stand as an unimaginable journey from a poor and unpromising point of departure. The rudiments of spiritual powers belonging to the gnostic Supernature are similarly there even in our ordinary composition, but only occasionally and sparsely active. It is not irrational to suppose that at this much higher stage of the evolution a similar but greater progression starting from these rudimentary beginnings might lead to another immense development and departure.

In mystic experience, — when there is an opening of the inner centres, or in other ways, spontaneously or by will or endeavour or in the very course of the spiritual growth, — new powers of consciousness have been known to develop; they present themselves as if an automatic consequence of some inner opening or in answer to a call in the being, so much so that it has been found necessary to recommend to the seeker not to hunt after these powers, not to accept or use them. This rejection is logical for those who seek to withdraw from life; for all acceptance of greater power would bind to life or be a burden on the bare and pure urge towards liberation. An indifference to all other aims and issues is natural for the God-lover who seeks God for His own sake and not for power or any other inferior attraction; the pursuit of these alluring but often dangerous forces would be a deviation from his purpose. A similar rejection is a necessary self-restraint and a spiritual discipline for the immature seeker, since such powers may be a great, even a deadly peril; for their supernormality may easily feed in him an abnormal exaggeration of the ego. Power in itself may be dreaded as a temptation by the aspirant to perfection, because power can abase as well as elevate; nothing is more liable to misuse. But when new capacities come as an inevitable result of the growth into a greater consciousness and a greater life and that growth is part of the very aim of the spiritual being within us, this bar does not operate; for a growth of the being into Supernature and its life in Supernature cannot take place or cannot be complete without bringing with it a greater power of consciousness and a greater power of life and the spontaneous development of an instrumentation of knowledge and force normal to that Supernature. There is nothing in this future evolution of the being which could be regarded as irrational or incredible; there is nothing in it abnormal or miraculous: it would be the necessary course of the evolution of consciousness and its forces in the passage from the mental to the gnostic or supramental formulation of our existence. This action of the forces of Supernature would be a natural, normal and spontaneously simple working of the new higher or greater consciousness into which the being enters in the course of his self-evolution; the gnostic being accepting the gnostic life would develop and use the powers of this greater consciousness, even as man develops and uses the powers of his mental nature.[1]

SRI AUROBINDO

... everyone has countless possibilities within him of which he is unaware and which develop only if he does what is to be done in the way it should be done.... But there are two types of progress, not only one; there is the progress that consists in perfecting more and more the capacities, possibilities, faculties and qualities you have — this is what is normally obtained by education; but if you go in for a little more thorough development by approaching a deeper truth, you can add, to the qualities you already have, other new ones which seem to be asleep in your being.

You can multiply your possibilities, enlarge and increase them; you can suddenly bring up something you did not think you had. I have already explained this to you several times. When one discovers one's psychic being within, at the same time there develop and manifest, quite unexpectedly, things one could not do at all before and which one didn't think were in one's nature. Of this too I have had numerous examples. I have given you this one, but I am repeating it to you once more to make myself understood.

I used to know a young girl who was born in a very ordinary environment, who had not received much education and wrote rather clumsy French, who had not developed her imagination and had absolutely no literary sense: that seemed to be among the possibilities she did not have. Well, when she had the inner experience of contact with her psychic being, and as long as the contact was living and very present, she wrote admirable things. When she fell back from that state into an ordinary one, she could not even put two sentences together correctly! And I saw examples of both kinds of her writing.

There is a genius within everyone of us — we don't know it. We must find the way to make it come out — but it is there sleeping, it asks for nothing better than to manifest; we must open the door to it.[2]   THE MOTHER

The field of our sense experience has an absolutely ridiculous limitation; while in the mind, if you think of someone or something, a city or a place, you are there immediately, instantaneously, you see. And you are there — it is not that you are not there, you are there, and you can have so precise a mental contact that you can have a conversation, ask questions and receive answers, on condition that the other person is fairly sensitive. Why, this is something which happens constantly, constantly. Only, you must have a little knowledge, naturally, for otherwise you don't even understand what is happening.

Even physically, with this, with the eyes, the nose, the fingers, the mouth, the ears, oh, it is ridiculous! One can develop these if one wants. One can succeed, for example, in hearing something which occurs at a fairly great distance and hearing it physically, not by another means than the physical, but one must have a control over his senses and be able to prolong their vibrations sufficiently. One can see at a distance also, and not by an occult vision. One can manage to stretch his vision, and if he knows how to prolong the vibration of his nerves outside the organ, he can prolong the contact, I don't say some kilometres away, no, but in a certain area, say, for example, through a wall, which is considered something impossible; one can see what is going on in a room which is separated from another by a wall. But a very methodical practice is necessary. Yet this is possible, seeing, feeling, hearing. If one wants to take the trouble, one can enlarge his field considerably. But it asks for work, for perseverance, a kind of assiduous effort. Why, it has even been found that one can develop other visual centres than the eye. It has been tried out with people who, for some reason or other, have no vision in the eye. One can develop other centres or another centre of vision, by a continuous, methodical effort. Jules Romains has written a book about it. He himself conducted experiments and obtained very conclusive results.

This means that we have a number of possibilities which we let sleep within us, because we don't take the trouble to develop them very much. We can do infinitely more than we actually do. But we take things like that, as they come.[3]

THE MOTHER

> *Sometimes there are latent powers in us of which we are unaware. To do a work, how is one to know whether one is capable of doing it or not?*

How can one know whether one is capable of doing it or not! By *trying*. That's the best thing. And if you do not succeed immediately, persevere. And you must know that if a strong urge, a very strong urge to do something comes to you, that means this work has something to do with you and you are capable of doing it. But one can have powers which are so well hidden that one has to dig long before finding them. So you must not get discouraged at the first setback, you must persist.[4]   THE MOTHER

POWER OF THOUGHT

Thoughts — Living and Conscious Formations

Thoughts are forms and have an individual life, independent of their author: sent out from him into the world, they move in it towards the realisation of their own purpose of existence. When you think of anyone, your thought takes a form and goes out to find him; and, if your thinking is associated with some will that is behind it, the thought-form that has gone out from you makes an attempt to realise itself. Let us say, for instance, that you have a keen desire for a certain person to come and that, along with this vital impulse of desire, a strong imagination accompanies the mental form you have made; you imagine, "If he came, it would be like this or it would be like that." After a time you drop the idea altogether, and you do not know that even after you have forgotten it, your thought continues to exist. For it does still exist and is in action, independent of you, and it would need a great power to bring it back from its work. It is working in the atmosphere of the person touched by it and creates in him the desire to come. And if there is a sufficient power of will in your thought-form, if it is a well-built formation, it will arrive at its own realisation. But between the formation and the realisation there is a certain lapse of time, and if in this interval your mind has been occupied with quite other things, then when there happens this fulfilment of your forgotten thought, you may not even remember that you once harboured it; you do not know that you were the instigator of its action and the cause of what has come about. And it happens very often too that when the result does come, you have ceased to desire or care for it. There are some men who have a very strong formative power of this kind and always they see their formations realised; but because they have not a well-disciplined mental and vital being, they want now one thing and now another and these different or opposite formations and their results collide and clash with one another. And these people wonder how it is that they are living in so great a confusion and disharmony! They do not realise that it is their own thoughts and desires that have built the circumstances around them which seem to them so incoherent and contradictory and make their life almost unbearable.[5]   THE MOTHER

You cannot think powerfully of something without your thought taking a form. But if you were to believe that this form was physical, that would obviously be an error, yet it really does exist in the mental world.[6]   THE MOTHER

When you have a thought, a well-made mental formation which goes out of you, it becomes an independent entity and continues on its way and it does that for which it was made. It continues to act independently of you. That is why you must be on your guard. If you have made such a formation and it has gone out, it has gone out to do its work; and after a time you find out that it was perhaps not a very happy thing to have a thought like that, that this formation was not very beneficial; now that it has gone out, it is very difficult for you to get hold of it again. You must have considerable occult knowledge. It has gone out and is moving on its way.... Supposing in a moment of great anger (I do not say that you do so, but still) when you were in quite a rage against someone, you said: "Ah! couldn't some misfortune befall him?" Your formation has gone on its way. It has gone out and you have no longer any control over it; and it goes and organises some misfortune or other: it is going to do its work. And after sometime the misfortune arrives. Happily, you do not usually have sufficient knowledge to tell yourself: "Oh! It is I who am responsible", but that is the truth.

Note that this power of formation has a great advantage, if one knows how to use it. You can make good formations and if you make them properly, they will act in the same way as the others. You can do a lot of good to people just by sitting quietly in your room, perhaps even more good than by undergoing a lot of trouble externally. If you know how to think correctly, with force and intelligence and kindness, if you love someone and wish him well very sincerely, deeply, with all your heart, that does him much good, much more certainly than you think. I have said this often; for example, to those who are here, who learn that someone in their family is very ill and feel that childish impulse of wanting to rush immediately to the spot to attend to the sick person. I tell you, unless it is an exceptional case and there is nobody to attend on the sick person (and at times even in such a case), if you know how to keep the right attitude and concentrate with affection and good will upon the sick person, if you know how to pray for him and make helpful formations, you will do him much more good than if you go to nurse him, feed him, help him wash himself, indeed all that everybody can do. Anybody can nurse a person. But

not everybody can make good formations and send out forces
that act for healing.[7]   THE MOTHER

> *Whatever an enemy may do to an enemy, whatever*
> *a hater may do to a hater, the harm caused by a*
> *misdirected mind is even greater still.*
>
> — The Dhammapada

... an ill-directed, ill-controlled thought does more harm than
an enemy can do to an enemy or a hater to a hater. That is
to say, even those who have the best intentions in the world,
if they do not have a wise control over their thought, will do
more harm to themselves and to those whom they love than
an enemy can do to an enemy or a hater to a hater.[8]

                                                  THE MOTHER

...one is surrounded by what one thinks about. You understand
quite well what this means? (*Turning to a child*) Every time
you think of something, it is as though you had a magnet in
your hand and were attracting that thing towards yourself —
you understand. Now, there are people who have a very, very
bad habit of always thinking about all possible catastrophes,
and are in a sort of constant apprehension about some calamity
befalling them the next moment. I know many like that, there
are some here. And so, those people have as though a magnet in
their hands to attract calamities, not only upon themselves but
upon others also. That lays a big responsibility upon them. And
if one can't stop all the time from thinking about something —
some have a head that runs on and they haven't found a way
of stopping it — well, why not make it run on the right lines

instead of letting it run on the others! Once your head begins to run, let it run on all the good things that can happen. If it is obliged to turn round and round, well, turn then to the good side! That is, if somebody is ill, instead of saying: "What is going to happen, perhaps this is going to be very serious, and if it is that disease... and a calamity comes so quickly", instead of all that, if one thinks:."Oh! that is nothing, illnesses are outer illusions translating some deeper vibrations which are not seen, that is why one doesn't speak about them, but that's how it is. And these deeper vibrations may come and set in order what has been disturbed. And this imbalance, this illness or bad thing that has come, well, it will be absorbed by the Grace and will disappear, no trace of it will remain, except that of things agreeable and pleasant." One may continue to think in this way uninterruptedly.... People always need to make their mind run, run, run, but then make it run on the right lines, you will see that it has an effect. For instance, let it go like this: that I shall learn better and better, shall know better and better, become healthier and healthier, and all difficulties will vanish, and wicked people will become sweet and good, and ill people will be cured, and houses which should be built will be built, and those things which should disappear will disappear, but giving place to better things, and the world will move in a constant progress, and at the end of that progress there will be a total harmony, and so on, and continue thus.... You can go on endlessly. But then you will have around you and around your head all kinds of pretty things. Those who perceive the atmosphere see certain inky stains, like an octopus there, yes, like that, with its tentacles to try and upset your mind — instead of that, one will see happy formations, formations of light or rays of sunlight or perhaps beautiful pictures, all

that. One will see beautiful things — there are painters who
do that and they always catch thoughts.[9]   THE MOTHER

Human thought is very creative in the mental world. All the
time when you are thinking, you are creating forms and you
send them out in the atmosphere and they go and do their work.
Constantly you are surrounded by a heap of small formations.

Naturally, there are people who can't even think clearly.
So they form nothing at all except faint eddies. But people who
think clearly are surrounded by a heap of little forms which,
sometimes, go out to do some work in others; and when one
thinks of them again, they return.

And we have instances of people who are troubled by
their own formations, which return constantly as though to
take possession of them, and which they can't get rid of because they don't know how to undo the formations they have
made. There are more cases of this kind than one would think.
When they have made a particularly strong formation — for
themselves, you see, relatively — this formation is always tied
up with the one who makes it and returns to knock at the brain
to receive forces and ends up by truly acting as a necessity. It
is a whole world to know; one truly lives in ignorance, one has
powers one doesn't know about, so naturally one uses them
very badly. One uses them somewhat unconsciously and very
badly.

I don't know if you have ever heard of Madame David-
Neel who went to Tibet and has written books on Tibet,
and who was a Buddhist; and Buddhists — Buddhists of the
strictest tradition — do not believe in the Divine, do not believe in his Eternity and do not believe in gods who are truly

divine, but they know admirably how to use the mental domain; and Buddhist discipline makes you a good master of the mental instrument and mental domain.

We used to discuss many things and once she told me: "Listen, I made an experiment." (She had studied a bit of theosophy also.) She said: "I formed a *mahatma*; with my thought I formed a *mahatma*." And she knew (this has been proved) that at a given moment mental formations acquire a personal life independent of the fashioner — though they are linked with him — but independent, in the sense that they can have their own will. And so she told me: "Just imagine, I had made my *mahatma* so well that he became a personality independent of me and constantly came to trouble me! He used to come, scold me for one thing, give me advice for another, and he wanted to direct my life; and I could not succeed in getting rid of him. It was extremely difficult, and I didn't know what to do!"

So I asked her how she had tried. She told me how. She said, "He troubles me a lot, my *mahatma* is very troublesome. He does not leave me in peace. He disturbs my meditations, he hinders me from working; and yet I know quite well that it is I who created him, and I can't get rid of him!" Then I said, "That's because you don't have the 'trick'...." (*Mother laughs*) And I explained to her what she should do. And the next day — I used to see her almost every day in those days, you see — the next day she came and told me, "Ah, I am freed from my *mahatma*!" (*Laughter*) She had not *cut* the connection because that's of no use. One must know how to *re-absorb* one's creation, that is the only way. To swallow up again one's formations.

But, you see, in a smaller measure and less perfectly one

is making formations all the time. When, for instance, one thinks of somebody quite powerfully, there is a small emanation of mental substance which, instantaneously, goes to this person, you understand, a vibration of your thought which goes and touches his; and if he is receptive, he sees you. He sees you and tells you, "You came last night to see me!" That's because you made a small formation and this formation went and did its work, which was to put you into contact with this person or else to carry a message if you had something special to tell him; and that was done. This happens constantly, but as it is quite a constant and spontaneous phenomenon and done in ignorance, one is not even aware that one does this, one does it automatically.

People who have desires add to the mental formation a kind of small envelope, a vital shell which gives it a still greater reality. These people are usually surrounded by a number of tiny entities which are their own formations, their own mental formations clothed with vital force, which come all the time to strike them to try to make them realise materially the formations they have made.

You have perhaps read the books of Maurice Magre; there are some in the library. He describes this; he had come here, Maurice Magre, and we spoke and he told me that he had always noticed — he was highly sensitive — he had always noticed that people who have sexual desires are surrounded by a kind of small swarm of entities who are somewhat viscous and rather ugly and which torment them constantly, awakening desire in them. He said he had seen this around certain people. It was like being surrounded by a swarm of mosquitoes, yes! But it is more gross, and much uglier still, and it is viscous, it is horrible, and it turns round and round the person and gives him no peace, and it awakens in him the desire that has formed these entities and they feast upon it. It is their food. This is absolutely true. His observation was quite correct. His vision was very true. It *is* like that.

But everyone carries around himself the atmosphere of his own desires. So you don't at all require that people should tell you anything; you have only to look and you see around them exactly the state they are in. They may want to give themselves the airs of angels or saints but they can't deceive you, because that thing is there, turning around them. So, just imagine! (*Mother points to all those seated in front of her.*) You see what you are like, how many of you there, all of you here, and each one has his own little world in this way, of mental formations of which some are clothed in vital substance, and all these crawl together, mix with each other, knock against each other. There is a struggle to see which is the strongest, which tries to realise itself, and all this creates an atmosphere indeed!...[10]   THE MOTHER

Occultism of Thought

... everybody practises occultism without knowing that he does. Everybody has this power spontaneously but doesn't know he has it. It may be a very slight one, like a pin-head; it may be as vast as the Earth or even the universe. But you cannot live without practising occultism, only you don't know it....

When you think — I have explained this to you I don't know how many times — when you think, you are practising occultism. Only, you don't know it. When you are thinking of someone, some part of you is automatically in contact with this person, and if to your thought is added a will that this person may be like this or like that or do this or that or understand this or that — whatever it may be — well, you are practising occultism, only you don't know it.... There are people who do this with power, and when they have a strong thought it manifests and is realised. There are people in whom it is very feeble and they do not obtain many results. It depends on the power of your thought and also on your power of concentration. But this kind of occultism everybody practises without even knowing it. So the difference from someone who really practises occultism is that he knows he is doing it and perhaps how he does it.[11]   THE MOTHER

[Written questions put to the Mother]

> *"Without conscious occult powers, is it possible to help or protect from a distance somebody in difficulty or danger? If so, what is the practical procedure?"*

Then a sub-question:

> *"What can thought do?"*

We are not going to speak of occult processes at all; although, to tell the truth, everything that happens in the invisible world is occult, by definition. But still, practically, there are two processes which do not exclude but complete each other, but which may be used separately according to one's preference.

It is obvious that thought forms a part of one of the methods, quite an important part. I have already told you several times that if one thinks clearly and powerfully, one makes a mental formation, and that every mental formation is an entity independent of its fashioner, having its own life and tending to realise itself in the mental world — I don't mean that you see your formation with your physical eyes, but it exists in the mental world, it has its own particular independent existence. If you have made a formation with a definite aim, its whole life will tend to the realisation of this aim. Therefore, if you want to help someone at a distance, you have only to formulate very clearly, very precisely and strongly the kind of help you want to give and the result you wish to obtain. That will have its effect. I cannot say that it will be all-powerful, for the mental world is full of innumerable formations of this kind and naturally they clash and contradict one another; hence the strongest and the most persistent will have the best of it.

Now, what is it that gives strength and persistence to mental formations? — It is emotion and will. If you know how to add to your mental formation an emotion, affection, tenderness, love, and an intensity of will, a dynamism, it will have a much greater chance of success. That is the first method. It is within the scope of all those who know how to think, and even more of those who know how to love. But as I said, the power is limited and there is great competition in that world.

Therefore, even if one has no knowledge at all but has trust in the divine Grace, if one has the faith that there is something in the world like the divine Grace, and that this something can answer a prayer, an aspiration, an invocation, then, after making one's mental formation, if one offers it to the Grace and puts one's trust in it, asks it to intervene and has the faith that it will intervene, then indeed one has a chance of success.

Try, and you will surely see the result.[12]   THE MOTHER

Power of Thought in Communication

... the ideal condition — which has already been partially realised by some people — is to transmit the essential idea and even something that is higher than the idea: the state — the state of consciousness, of knowledge, of perception — directly through the vibration. When you think, the mental substance vibrates in a certain way in accordance with the form your consciousness gives to your thought, and it is this vibration which should be perceived by the other mind if it is well attuned.

Indeed, words serve only to draw the attention of the other consciousness or the other centre of consciousness, so that it may be attentive to the vibration and receive it; but if it is not attentive and doesn't have the capacity to receive in comparative silence, you may pour out miles of words without making yourself understood in the least. And there comes a time when the brain, which is very active in emanating certain vibrations, can only receive vibrations which are clear and precise, otherwise it is a kind of vague mixture of something confused, imprecise, which gives the impression of a cloudy, woolly mass and doesn't evoke any idea. So one speaks, the sound is clearly heard, but it conveys nothing — it is not a question of sound, it is a matter of precision in the vibrations.

If you can emanate your thought in a very precise way, if it is something living and *conscious* emanating from your consciousness and going to meet the other consciousness, if, so to speak, you know what you want to say, then it arrives with the same precision, it awakens the corresponding vibration and with the corresponding vibration comes the corresponding thought or idea or state of consciousness, and you understand each other; but if what is emanated is woolly, imprecise, if you do not know very well what you want to say, if you yourself are trying to understand what you want to say, and if, on the other hand, the attention of the hearer is not alert enough or he is busy and active somewhere else, well then, you may talk to each other for hours, you will not understand each other at all!

And in fact this is what happens most often. When you are able to see in the consciousness of others the result of what you have tried to communicate, it always gives you the feeling of... you know what distorting mirrors are? Have you never seen distorting mirrors? Mirrors which make you look taller or fatter, which enlarge one part and reduce another, you are faced with a grotesque caricature of yourself — well, this is exactly what happens: in the other person's consciousness you have an altogether grotesque caricature of what you have said. And people imagine that they have understood each other because they have heard the sound of words, but they haven't communicated.

So, if you want to exercise the least effect on the mental substance, the first thing is to learn how to think clearly, and not a verbal thought which depends on words but a thought which can dispense with words, which can be understood in itself without words, which corresponds to a *fact*, the fact of a state of consciousness or a fact of knowledge. Just try to think without words, you will see where you stand.

Have you never tried it? Well then, try.

You have an absolutely clear and precise understanding of what you want to communicate to others — it vibrates in a special way, it has the power to give a form to the mental substance; and then, *afterwards*, as a concession to human habits you organise a certain number of words around it to try — there, much lower down — to give a verbal form to the vibration of consciousness. But the verbal form is entirely secondary. It is a kind of covering, a rather crude one, for the power of thought.[13]   THE MOTHER

Pre-Natal Moulding of an Infant

To bear a child and construct his body almost subconsciously is not enough. The work really commences when, by the power of thought and will, we conceive and create a character capable of manifesting an ideal.

And do not say that we have no power for realising such a thing. Innumerable instances of this very effective power could be brought out as proofs.

First of all, the effect of physical environment was recognised and studied long ago. It is by surrounding women with forms of art and beauty that, little by little, the ancient Greeks created the exceptionally harmonious race that they were.

Individual instances of the same fact are numerous. It is not rare to see a woman who, while pregnant, had looked at constantly and admired a beautiful picture or statue, giving birth to a child after the perfect likeness of this picture or statue. I met several of these instances myself. Among them, I remember very clearly two little girls; they were twins and perfectly beautiful. But the most astonishing was how little like their parents they were. They reminded me of a very famous picture painted by the English artist Reynolds. One day I made this remark to the mother, who immediately exclaimed: "Indeed, is it not so? You will be interested to know that while I was expecting these children, I had, hanging above my bed, a very good reproduction of Reynolds' picture. Before going to sleep and as soon as I woke, my last and first glance was for that picture; and in my heart I hoped: may my children be like the faces in this picture. You see that I succeeded quite well!" In truth, she could be proud of her success, and her example is of great utility for other women.

But if we can obtain such results on the physical plane where the materials are the least plastic, how much more so on the psychological plane where the influence of thought and will is so powerful. Why accept the obscure bonds of heredity and atavism — which are nothing else than subconscious preferences for our own trend of character — when we can, by concentration and will, call into being a type constructed according to the highest ideal we are able to conceive? With this effort, maternity becomes truly precious and sacred; indeed with this, we enter the glorious work of the Spirit, and womanhood rises above animality and its ordinary instincts, towards real humanity and its powers.[14]   THE MOTHER

Thought — as Instrument for Becoming

Thought is not essential to existence nor its cause, but it is an instrument for becoming; I become what I see in myself. All that thought suggests to me, I can do; all that thought reveals in me, I can become. This should be man's unshakable faith in himself, because God dwells in him.

Sri Aurobindo, *Thoughts and Glimpses*

... Sri Aurobindo declares that thought is not essential to existence, it is not the cause of existence, but is just the process, the instrument of becoming, for thought is a principle of precise formulation which has the power of creating forms. And as an illustration Sri Aurobindo says that all that one thinks one is, one can, by the very fact of that thinking, become. This knowledge of the fact that *all* that one thinks one can be, is a very important key for the development of the being, and not only from the point of view of the possibilities of the being, but also from that of the control and choice of what one will be, of what one wants to be.

This makes us understand the necessity of not admitting into ourselves any thought which destroys aspiration or the creation of the truth of our being. It reveals the considerable importance of not allowing what one doesn't want to be or doesn't want to do to formulate itself into thought within the being. Because to think these things is already a beginning of their realisation. From every point of view it is bad to concentrate on what one doesn't want, on what one has to reject, what one refuses to be, for the very fact that the thought is there gives to things one wants to reject a sort of right of existence within oneself. This explains the considerable importance of not letting destructive suggestions, thoughts of ill-will, hatred, destruction enter; for merely to think of them is already to give them a power of realisation. Sri Aurobindo says that thought is not the cause of existence but an intermediary, the instrument which gives form to life, to creation, and the control of this instrument is of foremost importance if one wants disorder and all that is anti-divine to disappear from creation.

One must not admit bad thoughts into oneself under the pretext that they are merely thoughts. They are tools of execution. And one should not allow them to exist in oneself if one doesn't want them to do their work of destruction.[15]

THE MOTHER

3

IMAGINATION

Imagination is a power of formation. In fact, people who have no imagination are not formative from the mental point of view, they cannot give a concrete power to their thought. Imagination is a very powerful means of action. For instance, if you have a pain somewhere and if you imagine that you are making the pain disappear or are removing it or destroying it — all kinds of images like that — well, you succeed perfectly.

There's a story of a person who was losing her hair at a fantastic rate, enough to become bald within a few weeks, and then someone told her, "When you brush your hair, imagine that it is growing and will grow very fast." And always, while brushing her hair, she said, "Oh! my hair is growing, oh! it will grow very fast.... " — And it happened! But what people usually do is to tell themselves, "Ah! all my hair is falling again and I shall become bald, that's certain, it's going to happen!"

And of course it happens![16]   THE MOTHER

How is it [disciplining the imagination] done?

Imagination is something very complex and manifold — what is vaguely called "imagination".

It can be the capacity for seeing and recording, noting the forms in some mental or other domain. There are artistic, literary, poetic domains, domains of action, scientific domains, all belonging to the mind — not a very high and abstract mind, a mind above the physical mind which, without our knowing it, pours out constantly through the individual and collective mind to manifest in action.

Some people, through a special faculty, are in contact with these domains, take up one formation or other that is there, draw them to themselves and give them an expression. This power of expression is different in different people, but those who can open themselves to these domains, to *see* things there, to draw these forms towards themselves and express them — either in literature or in painting or music or in action or science — are, according to the degree of their power of expression either very highly talented beings or else geniuses.

There are higher geniuses still. They are people who can open to a higher region, a higher force which, passing through the mental layers, comes and takes a form in a human mind and reveals itself in the world as new truths, new philosophical systems, new spiritual teachings, which are the works and at the same time the actions of the great beings who come to take birth on earth. That is an imagination which can be called "Truth-imagination".

These higher forces, when they come down into the earth-atmosphere, take living, active, powerful forms, spread throughout the world and prepare a new age.

These two kinds of imagination are what could be called higher imaginations.

And now, to come down to a more ordinary level, everyone has in him, in a greater or lesser measure, the power to give form to his mental activity and use this form either in his ordinary activity or to create and realise something. We are all the time, *always*, creating images, creating forms. We send them into the atmosphere without even knowing that we are doing so — they go roaming about, pass from one person to another, meet companions, sometimes join together and get on happily, sometimes create conflicts, and there are battles; for often, very often, in these mental imaginations there is a small element of will which tries to realise itself, and then everyone tries to send out his formation so that it can act, so that things can happen as he wants and, as everyone does this, it creates a general confusion. If our eyes were open to the vision of all these forms in the atmosphere, we would see very amazing things: battlefields, waves, onsets, retreats of a *crowd* of small mental entities which are constantly thrown out into the air and always try to realise themselves. All these formations have a common tendency to want to materialise and realise themselves physically, and as they are countless — they are far too many for there to be room enough on earth to manifest them — they jostle and elbow one another, they try to push back those which do not agree with them or even form armies marching in good order, always to take up the available room both in time and space — it is only a very small space compared with the countless number of creations.

So, individually, this is what happens. Some people do all that without knowing it — perhaps everybody — and they are constantly tossed from one thing to another, and hope, wish, desire, are disappointed, sometimes happy, sometimes in despair, for they don't have any control or mastery over these things. But the beginning of wisdom is to look at ourselves thinking and to see this phenomenon, become aware of this constant projection into the atmosphere of small *living* entities which are trying to manifest. All this comes out of the mental atmosphere which we carry within ourselves. Once we see and observe, we can begin to sort them out, that is, to push back what is not in conformity with our highest will or aspiration and allow to move towards manifestation only the formations which can help us to progress and develop normally.

This is the control of active thought, and that was what I meant the other day.

How many times you sit and become aware that the thought is beginning to form images for itself, to tell itself a story; and so, when you have become a little expert at it, not only do you see unfolding before you the history of what you would like to happen in life, in your own life, but you can take something away, add a detail, perfect your work, make a really *fine* story in which everything conforms with your highest aspiration. And once you have made a complete harmonious construction, as perfect as you can make it, then you open your hands and let the bird fly away.

If it is well made, it always realises itself in the end. And that is what one doesn't know.

But the thing is realised in the course of time, sometimes long afterwards, when you have forgotten your story, can no longer remember having told it to yourself — you have changed much, are thinking about other things, making other stories, and the first one no longer interests you; and if you are not very attentive, when the result of the first story comes, you are already very far away from it and no longer remember at all that this is the result of your own story.... And that is why it is so important to control yourself, for if within you there are multiple and contradictory wills — not only wills but tendencies, orientations, levels of life — all this causes battles in your life. For example, at your highest level you have fashioned a beautiful story which you send out into the world, but then, perhaps the next day, perhaps on the very same day, perhaps a little later, you have come down to a much more material level, and these things from above seem to you a little... fairylike, unreal; and you begin to make very concrete, very utilitarian formations which are not always very pretty... and these too go out.

I have known people with such opposite sides in their nature, so contradictory, that one day they could make a magnificent, luminous, powerful formation for realisation, and then the next day a defeatist, dark, black formation — a formation of despair — and so both would go out. And I was able to follow in the course of circumstances the beautiful one being realised, and while it was being realised, the dark one demolishing what the first one had done. And that is how it is in the larger lines of life as in its smaller details. And all that because one does not watch oneself thinking, because one believes one is the slave of these contradictory movements, because one says, "Oh! today I am not feeling well, oh! today things seem sad to me", and one says this as if it were an ineluctable fate against which one could do nothing. But if one stands back or ascends a step, one can look at all these things, put them in their place, keep some, destroy or get rid of those one does not want and put all one's imaginative power — what is called imaginative — only in those one wants and which conform with one's highest aspiration. That is what I call controlling one's imagination.

It is very interesting. When one learns to do it and does it regularly one no longer has time to feel bored.

And instead of being a cork afloat on the waves of the sea and tossed here and there by each wave, defencelessly, one becomes a bird which opens its wings, flies above the waves and goes wherever it wants.[17]   THE MOTHER

What is the function, the use of the imagination?

If one knows how to use it,... one can create for oneself his own inner and outer life; one can build his own existence with his imagination, if one knows how to use it and has a power. In fact it is an elementary way of creating, of forming things in the world. I have always felt that if one didn't have the capacity of imagination he would not make any progress. Your imagination always goes ahead of your life. When you think of yourself, usually you imagine what you want to be, don't you, and this goes ahead, then you follow, then it continues to go ahead and you follow. Imagination opens for you the path of realisation. People who are not imaginative — it is very difficult to make them move; they see just what is there before their nose, they feel just what they are moment by moment and they cannot go forward because they are clamped by the immediate thing. It depends a good deal on what one calls imagination. However...

Men of science must be having imagination!

A lot. Otherwise they would never discover anything. In fact, what is called imagination is a capacity to project oneself outside realised things and towards things realisable, and then to draw them by the projection. One can obviously have pro-gressive and regressive imaginations. There are people who always imagine all the catastrophes possible, and unfortu-nately they also have the power of making them come. It's like the antennae going into a world that's not yet realised, catching something there and drawing it here. Then naturally it is an addition to the earth atmosphere and these things tend towards manifestation. It is an instrument which can be disciplined, can be used at will; one can discipline it, direct it, orientate it. It is one of the faculties one can develop in himself and render serviceable, that is, use it for definite purposes.[18]

THE MOTHER

Then, is it through the imagination that one can realise desires or aspirations?

That means? What exactly do you want to say? Imagining that the desire is realised and in this way help its realisation?

Yes.

Certainly, quite certainly.

And ideals also?

Only usually, yes, almost totally what people don't have at their disposal is the time it takes. But for instance, if you have a very powerful imagination and build up the realisation of your desire, build it up well with all its details and everything, like an admirably made formation existing in itself, totally, you see... well, you may be sure that if you live long enough the thing will be realised. It can be realised the next day, it can be realised the next minute, it can take years, it can take centuries. But it is sure to be realised. And then, if to this imaginative power you add a kind of creative vital strength, you make a very living force of it; and as all living forces tend towards realisation, it will put a pressure upon terrestrial events in order to be able to realise itself sooner, and it is realised.

Only, as I said, there are two things. First, as regards desires, personal circumstances, one is not very... persistent or very steady, and after sometime what interested you very strongly doesn't interest you any longer. You think of something else, have another desire, and make another formation. But now the first thing one imagined is very well formed; after following its curve in space it is realised. But by then the person has started another construction because for some reason or other the thing doesn't interest him any more, and he is face to face with the realisation of his first desire, while having already embarked upon the second, the third or the fourth. So he is absolutely annoyed: "But why, I don't want this any longer, why does it come?" without his being conscious that quite simply it is the result of a previous deed. If, however, instead of being desires they are aspirations for spiritual things and one continues his line with a regular progress, then one is absolutely sure to obtain one day what he has imagined. The day may be slightly far-off if there are many obstacles on the path, for example if the formation that you have made is still very alien to the state of the earth atmosphere; well, it takes some time to prepare the conditions for its advent. But if it is something which has already been realised several times on earth and does not imply too categorical a transformation, you may have it quite quickly, provided that you follow the same line persistently. And if you add to this the ardour of a faith and trust in the divine Grace and that kind of self-giving to the Grace which makes you expect everything from It, then it can become tremendous; you can see things being realised more and more, and the most surprising ones can be realised one after another. But for this there are conditions to be fulfilled.[19]

THE MOTHER

The imagination is like a knife which may be used for good or evil purposes. If you always dwell in the idea and feeling that you are going to be transformed, then you will help the process of the Yoga. If, on the contrary, you give in to dejection and bewail that you are not fit or that you are incapable of realisation, you poison your own being.[20]   THE MOTHER

Childhood Dreams — Fashioners of the Future

... one must have a lively power of imagination, for — I seem to be telling you stupid things, but it is quite true — there is a world in which you are the supreme maker of forms: that is your own particular vital world. You are the supreme fashioner and you can make a marvel of your world if you know how to use it. If you have an artistic or poetic consciousness, if you love harmony, beauty, you will build there something marvellous which will tend to spring up into the material manifestation.

When I was small I used to call this "telling stories to oneself". It is not at all a telling with words, in one's head: it is a going away to this place which is fresh and pure, and... building up a wonderful story there. And if you know how to tell yourself a story in this way, and if it is truly beautiful, truly harmonious, truly powerful and well co-ordinated, this story will be realised in your life — perhaps not exactly in the form in which you created it, but as a more or less changed physical expression of what you made.

That may take years, perhaps, but your story will tend to organise your life.

But there are very few people who know how to tell a beautiful story; and then they always mix horrors in it, which they regret later.

If one could create a magnificent story without any horror in it, nothing but beauty, it would have a *considerable* influence on everyone's life. And this is what people don't know.

If one knew how to use this power, this creative power in the world of vital forms, if one knew how to use this while yet a child, a very small child... for it is then that one fashions his material destiny. But usually people around you, sometimes even your own little friends, but mostly parents and teachers, dabble in it and spoil everything for you, so well that very seldom does the thing succeed completely.

But otherwise, if it were done like that, with the spontaneous candour of a child, you could organise a wonderful life for yourself — I am speaking of the physical world.

The dreams of childhood are the realities of mature age.[21]

THE MOTHER

A Powerful Way of Self-Discovery

... when one goes on the discovery of one's inner being, of all the different parts of one's being, one very often has the feeling that one is entering deep into a hall or room, and according to the colour, the atmosphere, the things it contains, one has a very clear perception of the part of the being one is visiting. And then, one can go from one room to another, open doors and go into deeper and deeper rooms each of which has its own character. And often, these inner visits can be made during the night. Then it takes a still more concrete form, like a dream, and one feels that he is entering a house, and that this house is very familiar to him. And according to the time, the periods, it is internally different, and sometimes it may be in a state of very great disorder, very great confusion, where everything is mixed up; sometimes there are even broken things; it is quite a chaos. At other times these things are organised, put in their place; it is as though one had arranged the household, one cleans up, puts it in order, and it is always the same house. This house is the image, a kind of objective image, of your inner being. And in accordance with what you see there or do there, you have a symbolic representation of your psychological work. It is very useful for concretising. It depends on people.

Some people are just intellectuals; for them everything is expressed by ideas and not by images. But if they were to go down into a more material domain, well, they risk not touching things in their concrete reality and remaining only in the domain of ideas, remaining in the mind and remaining there indefinitely. Then one thinks one is making progress, and mentally one has done so, though it is something altogether indefinite.

The mind's progress may take thousands of years, for it is a very vast and very indefinite field, which is constantly renewed. But if one wants to progress in the vital and physical, well, this imaged representation becomes very useful for fixing the action, making it more concrete. Naturally it doesn't happen completely at will; it depends on each one's nature. But those who have the power of concentrating with images, well, they have one more facility.

To sit in meditation before a closed door, as though it were a heavy door of bronze — and one sits in front of it with the will that it may open — and to pass to the other side; and so the whole concentration, the whole aspiration is gathered into a beam and pushes, pushes, pushes against this door, and pushes more and more with an increasing energy until all of a sudden it bursts open, and one enters. It makes a very powerful impression. And so one is as though plunged into the light and then one has the full enjoyment of a sudden and radical change of consciousness, with an illumination that captures one entirely, and the feeling that one is becoming another person. And this is a very concrete and very powerful way of entering into contact with one's psychic being.[22]

THE MOTHER

4

CONCENTRATION

Concentration — the Master-Key

... whatever you may want to do in life, one thing is absolutely indispensable and at the basis of *everything*, the capacity of concentrating the attention. If you are able to gather together the rays of attention and consciousness on one point and can maintain this concentration with a persistent will, *nothing* can resist it — whatever it may be, from the most material physical development to the highest spiritual one. But this discipline must be followed in a constant and, it may be said, imperturbable way; not that you should always be concentrated on the same thing — that's not what I mean, I mean learning to concentrate.

And materially, for studies, sports, all physical or mental development, it is absolutely indispensable. And the value of an individual is proportionate to the value of his attention.

And from the spiritual point of view it is still more important. There is *no* spiritual obstacle which can resist a penetrating power of concentration. For instance, the discovery of the psychic being, union with the inner Divine, opening to the higher spheres, *all* can be obtained by an intense and obstinate power of concentration — but one must learn how to do it.

There is nothing in the human or even in the superhuman field, to which the power of concentration is not the key.

You can be the best athlete, you can be the best student, you can be an artistic, literary or scientific genius, you can be the greatest saint with that faculty. And everyone has in himself a tiny little beginning of it — it is given to everybody, but people do not cultivate it.[23]   THE MOTHER

... if your power of concentration is complete, then there is not a problem you cannot solve — I don't mean arithmetic problems (*laughter*), I mean problems about leading one's life, about decisions to be taken, psychological problems which need solving. There is not one that can resist this power of concentration.[24]   THE MOTHER

How is it that in people occupied with scientific studies artistic imagination is lacking? Are these two things opposed to each other?

Not necessarily.

In general?

They do not belong to the same domain. It is exactly as though you had what is called "a torchlight", a small beacon-light in your head at the place of observation. Scientists who want to do a certain work turn the beacon in a particular way, they always put it there and the beacon remains thus: they turn it towards matter, towards the details of matter. But people with imagination turn it upward, because up above there is everything, you know, all inspirations of artistic and literary things: this comes from another domain. It comes from a much more subtle domain, much less material. So these turn upward and want to receive the light from above. But it is the same instrument. The others turn it downwards, and it is just a lack of gymnastic skill. It is the same instrument. It is the same power of a luminous ray upon something. But as one has made it a habit of concentrating it in a certain direction, one is no longer supple, one loses the habit of doing things otherwise.

But you can at any time do both the things. When you are doing science, you turn it in one direction and when you do literature and art, you turn it in the other direction; but it is the same instrument: all depends on the orientation. If you have concentration, you can move this power of concentration from one place to another and in every way it will be effective. If you are occupied with science, you use it in a scientific way, and if you want to do art, you use it in an artistic way. But it is the same instrument and it is the same power of concentration. It is simply because people do not know this that they limit themselves. So the hinges get rusty, they do not turn any more. Otherwise, if one keeps the habit of turning them, they continue to turn. Moreover, even from the ordinary point of view, it is not rare to find a scientist having as his hobby some artistic occupation — and the reverse also. It is because they have found that the one was not harmful to the other and that it was the same faculty which could be utilised in both.

Essentially, from the general point of view, particularly from the intellectual viewpoint, the most important thing is the capacity of attention and concentration, it is that which one must work at and develop. From the point of view of action (physical action), it is the will: you must work and build up an unshakable will. From the intellectual point of view, you must work and build up a power of concentration which nothing can shake. And if you have both, concentration and will, you will be a genius and nothing will resist you.[25]   THE MOTHER

Gaining Time by Intensifying Concentration

When one works and wants to do one's best, one needs much time. But generally we don't have much time, we are in a hurry. How to do one's best when one is in a hurry?

It is a very interesting subject and I wanted to speak to you about it in detail, one day. Generally when men are in a hurry, they do not do completely what they have to do or they do badly what they do. Well, there is a third way, it is to intensify one's concentration. If you do that you can gain half the time, even from a very short time. Take a very ordinary example: to have your bath and to dress; the time needed varies with people, doesn't it? But let us say, half an hour is required for doing everything without losing time and without hurrying. Then, if you are in a hurry, one of two things happens: you don't wash so well or you dress badly! But there is another way — to concentrate one's attention and one's energy, think only of what one is doing and not of anything else, not to make a movement too much, to make the exact movement in the most exact way, and (it is an experience lived, I can speak of it with certitude) you can do in fifteen minutes what you were formerly doing in half an hour, and do it as well, at times even better, without forgetting anything, without leaving out anything, simply by the intensity of the concentration.

And this is the best answer to all those who say, "Oh, if one wants to do things well, one must have time." This is not true. For all that you do — study, play, work — there is only one solution: to increase one's power of concentration. And when you acquire this concentration, it is no longer tiring. Naturally, in the beginning, it creates a tension, but when you have grown used to it, the tension diminishes, and a moment comes when what fatigues you is to be not thus concentrated, to disperse yourself, allow yourself to be swallowed by all kinds of things, and not to concentrate on what you do. One can succeed in doing things even better and more quickly by the power of concentration. And in this way you can make use of work as a means of growth.[26]   THE MOTHER

When you work, if you are able to concentrate, you can do absolutely in ten minutes what would otherwise take you one hour. If you want to gain time, learn to concentrate. It is through attention that one can do things quickly and one does them much better. If you have a task that should take you half an hour — I don't say if you have to write for half an hour of course — but if you have to think and your mind is floating about, if you are thinking not only of what you are doing but also of what you have done and of what you will have to do and of your other subjects, all that makes you lose thrice as much time as you need to do your task. When you have too much to do, you must learn how to concentrate exclusively on what you are doing, with an intensity in your attention, and you can do in ten minutes what would otherwise take you one hour.[27]   THE MOTHER

... if you have much to do, you must learn how to concentrate much, all the more, and when you are doing a thing, to think of that only, and focus all your energy upon what you do. You gain at least half the time. So if you tell me: "I have too much work", I answer: "You do not concentrate enough."

> (Another child) *For a mathematical problem, sometimes the solution comes quickly, sometimes it takes too long.*

Yes, it is exactly that: it depends on the degree of concentration. If you observe yourself, you will notice this quite well: when it does not come, it is because of a kind of haziness in the brain, something cloudy, like a fog somewhere, and then you are there as in a dream. You push forward trying to find it, and it is as though you were pushing into cottonwool, you do not see clearly there; and so nothing comes. You may remain in that state for hours.

Concentration consists precisely in removing the cloud. You gather together all the elements of your intelligence and fix them on one point, and then you do not even try actively to find the thing. All that you do is to concentrate in such a way as to see only the problem — but seeing not only its surface, seeing it in its depth, what it conceals. If you are able to gather together all your mental energies, bringing them to a point which is fixed on the enunciation of the problem, and you stay there, fixed, as though you were about to drill a hole in the wall, all of a sudden it will come. And this is the only way. If you try: Is it this, is it that, is it this, is it that?... You will never find anything or else you will need hours. You must get your mental forces to a point with strength enough to pierce through the words and strike upon the thing that is behind. There is a thing to be found; swoop down upon it.[28]

THE MOTHER

There's a way of reducing the time necessary for doing things by increasing the concentration considerably. Some people can't do this for long, it tires them; but it's like weight-lifting, isn't it, one can get accustomed to it. And then, if you can suc-ceed in mastering this power of concentration and in making your mind absolutely still — for this indeed is the first condi-tion — and if in this quietude you concentrate it, concentrate, concentrate, concentrate on the point you want to make, on the work you have to do or the action you have to perform, well, you can... it comes like a kind of extremely quiet but all-powerful force of propulsion, and you go forward with one movement... without hesitation you can literally do in a quarter of an hour what would otherwise take one hour. And so this has the great advantage that it gives you time and that after this, instead of going from one activity to another, from one agitation to another, you can relax completely for some minutes and have a total rest. This gives you time to rest; and in this repose, naturally, as you are relaxed, all that could have been a little too tense is relaxed and put in order, and this puts you back in a condition in which you are once again able to make another concentration. [29]   THE MOTHER

Power of Spiritual Concentration

It is by the thought that we dissipate ourselves in the phe-nomenal; it is by the gathering back of the thought into itself that we must draw ourselves back into the real. Concentra-tion has three powers by which this aim can be effected. By concentration on anything whatsoever we are able to know that thing, to make it deliver up its concealed secrets; we must use this power to know not things, but the one Thing-in-itself. By concentration again the whole will can be gathered up for the acquisition of that which is still ungrasped, still beyond us; this power, if it is sufficiently trained, sufficiently single-minded, sufficiently sincere, sure of itself, faithful to itself alone, absolute in faith, we can use for the acquisition of any object whatsoever; but we ought to use it not for the acquisition of the many objects which the world offers to us, but to grasp spiritually that one object worthy of pursuit which is also the one subject worthy of knowledge. By concentration of our whole being on one status of itself, we can become whatever we choose; we can become, for instance, even if we were before a mass of weaknesses and fears, a mass instead of strength and courage, or we can become all a great purity, holiness and peace or a single universal soul of Love; but we ought, it is said, to use this power to become not even these things, high as they may be in comparison with what we now are, but rather to become that which is above all things and free from all action and attributes, the pure and absolute Being. All else, all other concentration can only be valuable for preparation, for previous steps, for a gradual training of the dissolute and self-dissipating thought, will and being towards their grand and unique object.[30]   SRI AUROBINDO

Powers of Concentration in the Three Centres

One can concentrate in any of the three centres which is easiest to the sadhak or gives most result. The power of the concentration in the heart-centre is to open that centre and by the power of aspiration, love, bhakti, surrender remove the veil which covers and conceals the soul and bring forward the soul or psychic being to govern the mind, life and body and turn and open them all fully to the Divine, removing all that is opposed to that turning and opening.

This is what is called in this yoga the psychic transformation. The power of concentration above the head is to bring peace, silence, liberation from the body sense, the identification with mind and life and open the way for the lower (mental, vital, physical) consciousness to rise up to meet the higher consciousness above and for the powers of the higher (spiritual nature) consciousness to descend into mind, life and body. This is what is called in this yoga the spiritual transformation. If one begins with this movement then the Power from above has in its descent to open all the centres (including the lowest centre) and to bring out the psychic being; for until that is done there is likely to be much difficulty and struggle of the lower consciousness obstructing, mixing with or even refusing the Divine Action from above. If the psychic being is once active this struggle and these difficulties can be greatly minimised.

The power of concentration in the eyebrows is to open the centre there, liberate the inner mind and vision and the inner or yogic consciousness and its experiences and powers. From here also one can open upwards and act also in the lower centres; but the danger of this process is that one may get shut up in one's mental spiritual formations and not come out of them into the free and integral spiritual experience and knowledge and integral change of the being and nature.[31]

SRI AUROBINDO

WILL-POWER

*When we have passed beyond willings, then we shall
have Power. Effort was the helper, Effort is the bar.*

Sri Aurobindo, Thoughts and Glimpses

And he contrasts these "willings" — that is, all these superficial wills, often opposite and contradictory and without any
lasting basis because they are founded on what he calls a
"knowing" and not on knowledge — with the true will. These
willings are necessarily fragmentary, passing, and often in
opposition to one another, and this is what gives to the individual life and even to the collective its nature of incoherence,
inconsistency and confusion.... The word "will" is normally
reserved to indicate what comes from the deeper being or the
higher reality and what expresses in action the true knowledge which Sri Aurobindo has contrasted with knowings. So,
when this will which expresses the true knowledge manifests
in action, it manifests through the intervention of a deep and
direct power which no longer requires any effort. And that is
why Sri Aurobindo says here that the true power for action
cannot come until one has gone beyond the stage of willings,
that is, until the motive of action is the result not of a mere
mental activity but of true knowledge.

True knowledge acting in the outer being gives true
power.

This seems to be an explanation, the real explanation
of that very familiar saying which is not understood in its

essence but expresses a truth: "Where there's a will, there's a way", to will is to have the power. It is quite obvious that this does not refer to "willings", that is, to the more or less incoherent expression of desires but to the true will expressing a true knowledge; for this true will carries in itself the force of truth which gives power — an invincible power. And so, when one expresses "willings", to be able to apply them in life and make them effective, some effort must come in — it is through personal effort that one progresses, and it is through effort that one imposes one's willings upon life to make it yield to their demands — but when they are no longer willings, when it is the true will expressing the true knowledge, effort is no longer required, for the power is omnipotent.[32]   THE MOTHER

> *Sweet Mother, how can we make our resolution very firm?*

By wanting it to be very firm! (*Laughter*)

No, this seems like a joke... but it is absolutely true. One does not want it truly. There is always, if you... It is a lack of sincerity. If you look sincerely, you will see that you have decided that it will be like this, and then, beneath there is something which has not decided at all and is waiting for the second of hesitation in order to rush forward. If you are sincere, if you are sincere and get hold of the part which is hiding, waiting, not showing itself, which knows that there will come a second of indecision when it can rush out and make you do the thing you have decided not to do...

But if you *really* want it, *nothing* in the world can prevent you from doing what you want. It is because one doesn't know how to will it. It is because one is *divided* in one's will. If you are not divided in your will, I say that nothing, nobody in the world can make you change your will.

But one doesn't know how to will it. In fact one doesn't even want to. These are velleities: "Well, it is like this.... It would be good if it were like that... yes, it would be better if it were like that... yes, it would be preferable if it were like that." But *this* is not to will. And always there at the back, hidden somewhere in a corner of the brain, is something which is looking on and saying, "Oh, why should I want that? After all one can as well want the opposite." And to try, you see... Not like that, just wait... But one can always find a thousand excuses to do the opposite. And ah, just a tiny little wavering is enough... pftt... the thing swoops down and there it is. But if one *wills,* if one really *knows* that *this* is the thing, and truly wants this, and if one is *oneself* entirely concentrated in the will, I say that there is *nothing* in the world that can prevent one from doing it, from doing it or being obliged to do it. It depends on what it is.

One wants. Yes, one wants, like this (*gestures*). One wants: "Yes, yes, it would be better if it were like that. Yes, it would be finer also, more elegant."... But, eh, eh, after all one is a weak creature, isn't that so? And then one can always put the blame upon something else: "It is the influence coming from outside, it is all kinds of circumstances."

The breath has passed, you see. You don't know... something... a moment of unconsciousness... "Oh, I was not conscious." You are not conscious because you do not accept... And all this because one doesn't know how to will.

To learn how to will is a very important thing. And to will truly, you must unify your being. In fact, to be a being, one must first unify oneself. If one is pulled by absolutely opposite tendencies, if one spends three-fourths of his life without being conscious of himself and the reasons why he does things, is one a real being? One does not exist. One is a mass of influences, movements, forces, actions, reactions, but one is not a being. One begins to become a being when he begins to have a will. And one can't have a will unless he is unified.

And when you have a will, you will be able to say, say to the Divine: "I want what You want." But not before that. Because in order to want what the Divine wants, you must have a will, otherwise you can will nothing at all. You would like to. You would like it very much. You would very much like to want what the Divine wants to do. You don't possess a will to give to Him and to put at His service. Something like that, gelatinous, like jelly-fish... there... a mass of good wills — and I am considering the better side of things and forgetting the bad wills — a mass of good wills, half-conscious and fluctuating.[33]

THE MOTHER

Power of Conscious Will Over the Body

The basis of all these methods [of physical culture] is the power exercised by the conscious will over matter. Usually it is a method which someone has used fairly successfully and set up as a principle of action, which he has taught to others who in turn have continued and perfected it until it has taken a somewhat fixed form of one kind of discipline or another. But the whole basis is the action of the conscious will on the body. The exact form of the method is not of primary importance. In various countries, at various times, one method or another has been used, but always behind it there is a canalised mental power which acts methodically. Of course, some methods try to use a higher power which would in its turn transmit its capacity to the mental power: if a power of a higher order is infused into the mental method, this method naturally becomes more effective and powerful. But essentially all these disciplines depend above all on the person who practises them and the way he uses them. One can, even in the most material, ordinary processes, make use of this altogether external basis to infuse into them powers of a higher order. And all methods, whatever they may be, depend almost exclusively on the person who uses them, on what he puts into them.

You see, if the matter is considered in its most modern, most external form, how is it that the movements we make almost constantly in our everyday life, or which we have to make in our work if it is a physical work, do not help or help very little, almost negligibly, to develop the muscles and to create harmony in the body? These same movements, on the other hand, if they are made consciously, deliberately, with a definite aim, suddenly start helping you to form your muscles and build up your body. There are jobs, for instance, where people have to carry extremely heavy loads, like bags of cement or sack⁻ of corn or coal, and they make a considerable effort; to a certain extent they do it with an acquired facility, but that doesn't give them harmony of the body, because they don't do it with the *idea* of developing their muscles, they do it just "like that". And someone who follows a method, either one he has learnt or one he has worked out for himself, and who makes these very movements with the will to develop this muscle or that, to create a general harmony in his body — he succeeds. Therefore, in the conscious will, there is something which adds considerably to the movement itself. Those who really want to practise physical culture as it is conceived now, everything they do, they do consciously. They walk downstairs consciously, they make the movements of ordinary life consciously, not mechanically. An attentive eye will perhaps notice a little difference but the greatest difference lies in the will they put into it, the consciousness they put into it. Walking to go somewhere and walking as an exercise is not the same thing. It is the conscious will in all these things which is important, it is that which brings about the progress and obtains the result. Therefore, what I mean is that the method one uses has only a relative importance in itself; it is the will to obtain a certain result that is important.

The yogi or aspiring yogi who does *asanas* to obtain a spiritual result or even simply a control over his body, obtains these results because it is with this aim that he does them, whereas I know some people who do exactly the same things but for all sorts of reasons unrelated to spiritual development, and who haven't even managed to acquire good health by it! And yet they do exactly the same thing, sometimes they even do it much better than the yogi, but it doesn't give them a stable health... because they haven't thought about it, haven't done it with this purpose in mind. I have asked them myself, I said, "But how can you be ill after doing all that?" — "Oh! but I never thought of it, that's not why I do it." This amounts to saying that it is the conscious will which acts on matter, not the material fact.

But you only have to try it, you will understand very well what I mean. For instance, all the movements you make when dressing, taking your bath, tidying your room... no matter what; make them consciously, with the will that this muscle should work, that muscle should work. You will see, you will obtain really amazing results.

Going up and down the stairs — you cannot imagine how useful that can be from the point of view of physical culture, if you know how to make use of it. Instead of going up because you are going up and coming down because you are coming down, like any ordinary man, you go up with the consciousness of all the muscles which are working and of making them work harmoniously. You will see. Just try a little, you will see! This means that you can use all the movements of your life for a harmonious development of your body.

You bend down to pick something up, you stretch up to find something right at the top of a cupboard, you open a door, you close it, you have to go round an obstacle, there are a hundred and one things you do constantly and which you can make use of for your physical culture and which will demonstrate to you that it is the consciousness you put into it which produces the effect, a hundred times more than just the material fact of doing it. So, you choose the method you like best, but you can use the whole of your daily life in this way.... To think constantly of the harmony of the body, of the beauty of the movements, of not doing anything that is ungraceful and awkward. You can obtain a rhythm of movement and gesture which is very exceptional.[34]   THE MOTHER

6

FAITH

Faith and Cure

It is not the medicine that cures so much as the patient's faith in the doctor and the medicine. Both are a clumsy substitute for the natural faith in one's own self-power which they have themselves destroyed.[35]

SRI AUROBINDO

These auto-suggestions — it is really faith in a mental form — act both on the subliminal and the subconscient. In the subliminal they set in action the powers of the inner being, its occult power to make thought, will or simple conscious force effective on the body — in the subconscient they silence or block the suggestions of death and illness (expressed or unexpressed) that prevent the return of health. They help also to combat the same things (adverse suggestions) in the mind, vital, body consciousness. Where all this is completely done or with some completeness, the effects can be very remarkable.[36]

SRI AUROBINDO

We laugh at the savage for his faith in the medicine man; but how are the civilised less superstitious who have faith in the doctors? The savage finds that when a certain incantation is repeated, he often recovers

*from a certain disease; he believes. The civilised pa-
tient finds that when he doses himself according to a
certain prescription, he often recovers from a certain
disease; he believes. Where is the difference?*

Sri Aurobindo, *Thoughts and Aphorisms*

One could say in conclusion that it is the faith of the patient
which gives the remedy its power to heal.

If men had an absolute faith in the healing power of
Grace, they would perhaps avoid many illnesses.[37]

THE MOTHER

*Mother, by a mental effort — for instance, the resolu-
tion not to take medicines when one is ill — can one
succeed in making the body understand?*

That is not enough. A mental resolution is not enough, no.
There are subtle reactions in your body which do not obey the
mental resolution, it is not enough. Something else is needed.

Other regions must be contacted. A power higher than
the mind's is needed....

No, it is not in the mental field that the victories are won.
It is impossible. It is open to all influences, all contradictory
currents. All the mental constructions one makes carry their
own contradiction with them. One can try to overrule it or
make it as harmless as possible, but it exists, it is there, and
at the slightest weakness or lack of vigilance or inadvertance,
it enters, and destroys all the work. Mentally, one arrives at
very few results, and they are always mixed. Something else
is needed. One must pass from the mind into the domain of
faith or of a higher consciousness, to be able to act with safety.

It is quite obvious that one of the most powerful means for acting on the body is faith. People who have a simple heart, not a very complicated mind — simple people, you see — who don't have a very great, very complicated mental development but have a very deep faith, have a great power of action over their bodies, very great. That is why one is quite surprised at times: "Here's a man with a great realisation, an exceptional person, and he is a slave of all the smallest physical things, while this man, well, he is so simple and looks so uncouth, but he has a great faith and goes through difficulties and obstacles like a conqueror!"

I don't say that a highly cultured man can't have faith, but it is more difficult, for there is always this mental element which contradicts, discusses, tries to understand, which is difficult to convince, which wants proofs. His faith is less pure. It is necessary, then, to pass on to a higher degree in the evolutionary spiral, pass from the mental to the spiritual; then, naturally, faith takes on a quality of a very high order. But I mean that in daily life, ordinary life, a very simple man who has a very ardent faith can have a mastery over his body — without it being truly a "mastery"; it is simply a spontaneous movement — a control over his body far greater than somebody who has reached a much higher development.[38]

THE MOTHER

Integral Faith

Can mere faith create all, conquer all?

Yes, but it must be an integral faith and it must be absolute.

And it must be of the right kind, not merely a force of mental thought or will, but something more and deeper. The will put forth by the mind sets up opposite reactions and creates a resistance. You must have heard something of the method of Coué in healing diseases. He knew some secret of this power and utilised it with considerable effect; but he called it imagination and his method gave the faith he called up too mental a form. Mental faith is not sufficient; it must be completed and enforced by a vital and even a physical faith, a faith of the body. If you can create in yourself an integral force of this kind in all your being, then nothing can resist it; but you must reach down to the most subconscious, you must fix the faith in the very cells of the body.[39]   THE MOTHER

Faith and Confidence

Long ago some people used to believe that a perforated coin... It was in the days when coins were not perforated... now we have perforated coins, don't we, some countries have perforated coins, but in those days they were not perforated, and yet sometimes there were holes in a coin. And there was indeed a superstition like this, that when one found a perforated coin, it brought good luck. It brought you good luck and success in what you wanted to do.

There was a man working in an office whose life was rather poor and who was not very successful, and one day he found a perforated coin. He put it in his pocket and said to himself, "Now I am going to prosper!" And he was full of hope, courage, energy, because he knew: "Now that I have the coin, I am sure to succeed!" And, in fact, he went on prospering, prospering more and more. He earned more and more money, he had a better and better position, and people said, "What a wonderful man! How well he works! How he finds all the solutions to all problems!" Indeed, he became a remarkable man, and every morning when he put on his coat, he felt it — like this — to be sure that his coin was in his pocket.... He touched it, he felt that the coin was there, and he had confidence. And then, one day, he was a little curious, and said, "I am going to see my coin!" — years later. He was having his breakfast with his wife and said, "I am going to see my coin!" His wife told him, "Why do you want to see it? It's not necessary." "Yes, yes, let me see my coin." He took out the little bag in which he kept the coin, and found inside a coin which was not perforated!

"Ah," he said, "this is not my coin! What is this? Who has changed my coin?" Then his wife told him, "Look, one day there was some dust on your coat.... I shook it off through the window and the coin fell out. I had forgotten that the coin was there. I ran to look for it but didn't find it. Someone had picked it up. So I thought you would be very unhappy and I put another coin there." (*Laughter*) Only, he, of course, was confident that his coin was there and that was enough.

It is the faith, the trust that does it, you see.... The perforated coin gives you nothing at all. You can always try. If you have the confidence, it gives you... When one has confidence...[40]   THE MOTHER

Faith and Trust

A dynamic faith and a great trust, aren't they the same thing?

Not necessarily. One should know of what stuff the faith and the trust are made. Because, for instance, if you live normally, under quite normal conditions — without having extravagant ideas and a depressing education — well, through all your youth and usually till you are about thirty, you have an absolute trust in life. If, for example, you are not surrounded by people who, as soon as you have a cold in the head, get into a flurry and rush to the doctor and give you medicines, if you are in normal surroundings and happen to have something — an accident or a slight illness — there is this certainty in the body, this absolute trust that it will be all right: "It is nothing, it will pass off. It is sure to go. I shall be quite well tomorrow or in a few days. It will surely be cured" — whatever you may have caught. That is indeed the normal condition of the body. An absolute trust that all life lies before it and that all will be well. And this helps enormously. One gets cured nine times out of ten, one gets cured very quickly with this confidence: "It is nothing; what is it after all? Just an accident, it will pass off, it is nothing." And there are people who keep it for a very long time, a very long time, a kind of confidence — nothing can happen to them. Their life is all before them, fully, and nothing can happen to them. And what will happen to them is of no importance at all: all will be well, perforce; they have the whole of life before them. Naturally, if you live in surroundings where there are morbid ideas and people pass their time recounting disastrous and catastrophic things, then you may think wrongly. And if you think wrongly, this reacts on your body. Otherwise, the body as it is can keep this confidence till the age of forty or fifty — it depends upon people — some know how to live a normal, balanced life. But the body is quite confident about its life. It is only if thought comes in and brings all kinds of morbid and unhealthy imaginations, as I said, that it changes everything. I have seen instances like that: children who had these little accidents one has when running and playing about: they did not even think about it. And it disappeared immediately. I have seen others whose family has drummed into them since the time they could understand, that everything is dangerous, that there are microbes everywhere, that one must be very careful, that the least wound may prove disastrous, that one must be altogether on one's guard and take great care that nothing serious happens.... So, they must have their wounds dressed, must be washed with disinfectants, and there they sit wondering: "What is going to happen to me? Oh! I may perhaps get tetanus, a septic fever...." Naturally, in such cases one loses confidence in life and the body feels the effects keenly. Three-fourths of its resistance disappears. But normally, naturally, it is the body which knows that it must remain healthy, and it knows it has the power to react. And if something happens, it tells this something: "It is nothing, it will go away, don't think about it, it is over"; and it does go.

That of course is absolute trust.

Now, you are speaking of "dynamic faith". Dynamic faith is something different. If one has within him faith in the divine grace, that the divine grace is watching over him, and that no matter what happens the divine grace is there, watching over him, this one may keep all one's life and always; and with this one can pass through all dangers, face all difficulties, and nothing stirs, for you have the faith and the divine grace is with you. It is an infinitely stronger, more conscious, more lasting force which does not depend upon the conditions of your physical build, does not depend upon anything except the divine grace alone, and hence it leans on the Truth and nothing can shake it. It is very different.[41]   THE MOTHER

What are the conditions in which there is a descent of faith?

The most important condition is an almost childlike trust, the candid trust of a child who is sure that it will come, who doesn't even ask himself about it; when he needs something he is sure that it is going to come. Well, it is this, this kind of trust — this indeed is the most important condition.

To aspire is indispensable. But some people aspire with such a conflict inside them between faith and absence of faith, trust and distrust, between the optimism which is sure of victory and a pessimism which asks itself when the catastrophe will come. Now if this is in the being, you may aspire but you don't get anything. And you say, "I aspired but didn't get anything." It is because you demolish your aspiration all the time by your lack of confidence. But if you truly have trust... Children when left to themselves and not deformed by older people have such a great trust that all will be well! For example, when they have a small accident, they never think that this is going to be something serious: they are spontaneously convinced that it will soon be over, and this helps so powerfully in putting an end to it.

Well, when one aspires for the Force, when one asks the Divine for help, if one asks with the unshakable certitude that it will come, that it is impossible that it won't, then it is sure to come. It is this kind... yes, this is truly an inner opening, this trustfulness. And some people are constantly in this state. When there is something to be received, they are always there to receive it. There are others, when there is something to have, a force descends, they are always absent, they are always closed at that moment; while those who have this childlike trust are always there at the right time.

And it is strange, isn't it, outwardly there is no difference. They may have exactly the same goodwill, the same aspiration, the same wish to do good, but those who have this smiling confidence within them, do not question, do not ask themselves whether they will have it or not have it, whether the Divine will answer or not — the question does not arise, it is something understood... "What I need will be given to me; if I pray I shall have an answer; if I am in a difficulty and ask for help, the help will come — and not only will it come but it will manage everything." If the trust is there, spontaneous, candid, unquestioning, it works better than anything else, and the results are marvellous. It is with the contradictions and doubts of the mind that one spoils everything, with this kind of notion which comes when one is in difficulties: "Oh, it is impossible! I shall never manage it. And if it is going to be aggravated, if this condition I am in, which I don't want, is going to grow still worse, if I continue to slide down farther and farther, if, if, if, if... " like that, and one builds a wall between oneself and the force one wants to receive. The psychic being has this trust, has it wonderfully, without a shadow, without an argument, without a contradiction. And when it is like that, there is not a prayer which does not get an answer, no aspiration which is not realised.[42]   THE MOTHER

Increasing One's Faith

Sweet Mother, can faith be increased by personal effort?

Faith is certainly a gift given to us by the Divine Grace. It is like a door suddenly opening upon an eternal truth, through which we can see it, almost touch it.

As in everything else in the ascent of humanity, there is the necessity — especially at the beginning — of personal effort. It is possible that in some exceptional circumstances, for reasons which completely elude our intelligence, faith may come almost accidentally, quite unexpectedly, almost without ever having been solicited, but most frequently it is an answer to a yearning, a need, an aspiration, something in the being that is seeking and longing, even though not in a very conscious and systematic way. But in any case, when faith has been granted, when one has had this sudden inner illumination, in order to preserve it constantly in the active consciousness individual effort is altogether indispensable. One must *hold on* to one's faith, *will* one's faith; one must seek it, cultivate it, protect it.

In the human mind there is a morbid and deplorable habit of doubt, argument, scepticism. *This* is where human effort must be put in: the refusal to admit them, the refusal to listen to them and still more the refusal to follow them. No game is more dangerous than playing mentally with doubt and scepticism. They are not only enemies, they are terrible pitfalls, and once one falls into them, it becomes tremendously difficult to pull oneself out.

Some people think it is a very great mental elegance to play with ideas, to discuss them, to contradict their faith; they think that this gives them a very superior attitude, that in this way they are above "superstitions" and "ignorance"; but if you listen to suggestions of doubt and scepticism, *then* you fall into the grossest ignorance and stray away from the right path. You enter into confusion, error, a maze of contradictions.... You are not always sure you will be able to get out of it. You go so far away from the inner truth that you lose sight of it and sometimes lose too all possible contact with your soul.

Certainly a personal effort is needed to preserve one's faith, to let it grow within. Later — much later — one day, looking back, we may see that everything that happened, even what seemed to us the worst, was a Divine Grace to make us advance on the way; and then we become aware that the personal effort too was a grace. But before reaching that point, one has to advance much, to struggle much, sometimes even to suffer a great deal.

To sit down in inert passivity and say, "If I am to have faith I shall have it, the Divine will give it to me", is an attitude of laziness, of unconsciousness and almost of bad-will.

For the inner flame to burn, one must feed it; one must watch over the fire, throw into it the fuel of all the errors one wants to get rid of, all that delays the progress, all that darkens the path. If one doesn't feed the fire, it smoulders under the ashes of one's unconsciousness and inertia, and then, not years but lives, centuries will pass before one reaches the goal.

One must watch over one's faith as one watches over the birth of something *infinitely* precious, and protect it very carefully from everything that can impair it.

In the ignorance and darkness of the beginning, faith is the most direct expression of the Divine Power which comes to fight and conquer.[43]   THE MOTHER

7

ATTITUDE

If, in the presence of circumstances that are about to take place, you can take the highest attitude possible — that is, if you put your consciousness in contact with the highest consciousness within reach, you can be absolutely sure that in that case it is the best that can happen to you. But as soon as you fall from this consciousness into a lower state, then it is evidently not the best that can happen, for the simple reason that you are not in your very best consciousness. I even go so far as to affirm that in the zone of immediate influence of each one, the right attitude not only has the power to turn every circumstance to advantage but can change the very circumstance itself. For instance, when a man comes to kill you, if you remain in the ordinary consciousness and get frightened out of your wits, he will most probably succeed in doing what he came for; if you rise a little higher and though full of fear call for the divine help, he may just miss you, doing you a slight injury; if, however, you have the right attitude and the full consciousness of the divine presence everywhere around you, he will not be able to lift even a finger against you....

I have had innumerable examples of the power of right attitude. I have seen crowds saved from catastrophes by one single person keeping the right attitude. But it must be an attitude that does not remain somewhere very high and leaves the body to its usual reactions. If you remain high up like that, saying, "Let God's will be done", you may get killed all the same. For your body may be quite undivine, shivering with fear: the thing is to hold the true consciousness in the body itself and not have the least fear and be full of the divine peace. Then indeed there is no danger. Not only can attacks of men be warded off, but beasts also and even the elements can be affected.[44]   THE MOTHER

Sincerity

... there are people who tell me, "I don't have the will-power [to overcome desire]." That means you are not sincere. For sincerity is an infinitely more powerful force than all the wills in the world. It can change anything whatever in the twinkling of an eye; it takes hold of it, grips it, pulls it out — and then it's over.

But you close your eyes, you find excuses for yourself.[45]

THE MOTHER

Sincerity is the safeguard, the protection, the guide, and finally the transforming power.[46]   THE MOTHER

Endurance

Let endurance be your watchword: teach the life-force in you — your vital being — not to complain but to put up with all the conditions necessary for great achievement. The body is a very enduring servant, it bears the stress of circumstance tamely like a beast of burden. It is the vital being that is always grumbling and uneasy. The slavery and torture to which it subjects the physical is almost incalculable. How it twists and deforms the poor body to its own fads and fancies, irrationally demanding that everything should be shaped according to its whimsicality! But the very essence of endurance is that the vital should learn to give up its capricious likes and dislikes and preserve an equanimity in the midst of the most trying conditions. When you are treated roughly by somebody or you lack something which would relieve your discomfort, you must keep up cheerfully instead of letting yourself be disturbed. Let nothing ruffle you the least bit, and whenever the vital tends to air its petty grievances with pompous exaggeration just stop to consider how very happy you are, compared to so many in this world. Reflect for a moment on what the soldiers who fought in the last war had to go through. If you had to bear such hardships you would realise the utter silliness of your dissatisfactions. And yet I do not wish you to court difficulties — what I want is simply that you should learn to endure the little insignificant troubles of your life.

Nothing great is ever accomplished without endurance. If you study the lives of great men you will see how they set themselves like flint against the weaknesses of the vital. Even today, the true meaning of our civilisation is the mastery of the physical through endurance in the vital. The spirit of sport and of adventure and the dauntless facing of odds which is evident in all fields of life are part of this ideal of endurance. In science itself, progress depends on the countless difficult tests and trials which precede achievement.... What you must do is to give your vital a good beating as soon as it protests; for, when the physical is concerned, there is reason to be considerate and to take precautions, but with the vital the only method is a sound "kicking". Kick your vital the moment it complains, because there is no other way of getting out of the petty consciousness which attaches so much importance to creature comforts and social amenities instead of asking for the Light and the Truth.[47]   THE MOTHER

The body has a remarkable capacity of adaptation and endurance. It is fit to do so many more things than one can usually imagine. If instead of the ignorant and despotic masters that govern it, it is ruled by the central truth of the being, one will be surprised at what it is capable of doing.

The Mother, "The Science of Living", *On Education*

During the last war, it was proved that the body was capable of enduring such suffering as is normally impossible to endure. You have surely read or heard these stories of war in which the body was made to suffer and endure terrible things, and it withstood all that, it proved that it had almost inexhaustible capacities of endurance. Some people happened to be under conditions that should have killed them; if they survived, it was because they had in them a very strong will to survive and the body obeyed that will.[48]   THE MOTHER

The principle of endurance relies on the strength of the spirit within us to bear all the contacts, impacts, suggestions of this phenomenal Nature that besieges us on every side without being overborne by them and compelled to bear their emotional, sensational, dynamic, intellectual reactions. The outer mind in the lower nature has not this strength. Its strength

is that of a limited force of consciousness which has to do
the best it can with all that comes in upon it or besieges it
from the greater whirl of consciousness and energy which
environs it on this plane of existence. That it can maintain
itself at all and affirm its individual being in the universe, is
due indeed to the strength of the spirit within it, but it cannot
bring forward the whole of that strength or the infinity of
that force to meet the attacks of life; if it could, it would
be at once the equal and master of its world. In fact, it has
to manage as it can. It meets certain impacts and is able to
assimilate, equate or master them partially or completely, for
a time or wholly, and then it has in that degree the emotional
and sensational reactions of joy, pleasure, satisfaction, liking,
love, etc., or the intellectual and mental reactions of acceptance, approval, understanding, knowledge, preference, and
on these its will seizes with attraction, desire, the attempt to
prolong, to repeat, to create, to possess, to make them the
pleasurable habit of its life. Other impacts it meets, but finds
them too strong for it or too dissimilar and discordant or too
weak to give it satisfaction; these are things which it cannot
bear or cannot equate with itself or cannot assimilate, and it
is obliged to give to them reactions of grief, pain, discomfort,
dissatisfaction, disliking, disapproval, rejection, inability to
understand or know, refusal of admission. Against them it
seeks to protect itself, to escape from them, to avoid or min-
imise their recurrence; it has with regard to them movements of
fear, anger, shrinking, horror, aversion, disgust, shame, would
gladly be delivered from them, but it cannot get away from
them, for it is bound to and even invites their causes and
therefore the results; for these impacts are part of life, tangled
up with the things we desire, and the inability to deal with

them is part of the imperfection of our nature. Other impacts again the normal mind succeeds in holding at bay or neutralising and to these it has a natural reaction of indifference, insensibility or tolerance which is neither positive acceptance and enjoyment nor rejection or suffering. To things, persons, happenings, ideas, workings, whatever presents itself to the mind, there are always these three kinds of reaction. At the same time, in spite of their generality, there is nothing absolute about them; they form a scheme for a habitual scale which is not precisely the same for all or even for the same mind at different times or in different conditions. The same impact may arouse in it at one time and another the pleasurable or positive, the adverse or negative or the indifferent or neutral reactions.

The soul which seeks mastery may begin by turning upon these reactions the encountering and opposing force of a strong and equal endurance. Instead of seeking to protect itself from or to shun and escape the unpleasant impacts it may confront them and teach itself to suffer and to bear them with perseverance, with fortitude, an increasing equanimity or an austere or calm acceptance. This attitude, this discipline brings out three results, three powers of the soul in relation to things. First, it is found that what was before unbearable, becomes easy to endure; the scale of the power that meets the impact rises in degree; it needs a greater and greater force of it or of its protracted incidence to cause trouble, pain, grief, aversion or any other of the notes in the gamut of the unpleasant reactions. Secondly, it is found that the conscious nature divides itself into two parts, one of the normal mental and emotional nature in which the customary reactions continue to take place, another of the higher will and reason which observes and is not troubled or affected by the passion of this lower nature, does not accept it as its own, does not approve, sanction or participate. Then the lower nature begins to lose the force and power of its reactions, to submit to the suggestions of calm and strength from the higher reason and will, and gradually that calm and strength take possession of the mental and emotional, even of the sensational, vital and physical being. This brings the third power and result, the power by this endurance and mastery, this separation and rejection of the lower nature, to get rid of the normal reactions and even, if we will, to remould all our modes of experience by the strength of the spirit. This method is applied not only to the unpleasant, but also to the pleasant reactions; the soul refuses to give itself up to or be carried away by them; it endures with calm the impacts which bring joy and pleasure; refuses to be excited by them and replaces the joy and eager seeking of the mind after pleasant things by the calm of the spirit. It can be applied too to the thought-mind in a calm reception of knowledge and of limitations of knowledge which refuses to be carried away by the fascination of this attractive or repelled by dislike for that unaccustomed or unpalatable thought-suggestion and waits on the Truth with a detached observation which allows it to grow on the strong, disinterested, mastering will and reason. Thus the soul becomes gradually equal to all things, master of itself, adequate to meet the world with a strong front in the mind and an undisturbed serenity of the spirit.[49]

SRI AUROBINDO

Cheerfulness

Another remarkable sign of the conversion of your vital, ow-
ing to Agni's influence, is that you face your difficulties and
obstacles with a smile. You do not sit any more in sackcloth
and ashes, lamenting over your mistakes and feeling utterly
crestfallen because you are not at the moment quite up to
the mark. You simply chase away depression with a smile.
A hundred mistakes do not matter to you: with a smile you
recognise that you have erred and with a smile you resolve
not to repeat the folly in the future. All depression and gloom
is created by the hostile forces who are never so pleased as
when throwing on you a melancholy mood. Humility is indeed
one thing and depression quite another, the former a divine
movement and the latter a very crude expression of the dark
forces. Therefore, face your troubles joyously, oppose with
invariable cheerfulness the obstacles that beset the road to
transformation. The best means of routing the enemy is to
laugh in his face! You may grapple and tussle for days and he
may still show an undiminished vigour; but just once laugh at
him and lo! he takes to his heels. A laugh of self-confidence
and of faith in the Divine is the most shattering strength possible — it disrupts the enemy's front, spreads havoc in his ranks
and carries you triumphantly onwards.[50]   THE MOTHER

Awakened Consciousness

There is a moment for choice, even in an accident. For instance, one slips and falls. Just between the moment one has
slipped and the moment one falls there is a fraction of a second.

At that moment one has the choice: it may be nothing much, it may be very serious. Only, the consciousness must naturally be wide awake and one must be in contact with one's psychic being constantly — there is no time to make the contact, one must *be* in contact. Between the moment one slips and the moment one is on the ground, if the mental and psychic formation is sufficiently strong, then there is nothing, nothing will happen — nothing happens. But if at that moment, the mind according to its habit becomes a pessimist and tells itself: "Oh! I have slipped.... " That lasts the fraction of a second; that doesn't take even a minute, it is a fraction of a second; during a fraction of a second one has the choice. But one must be so awake, every minute of one's life! For a fraction of a second one has the choice, there is a fraction of a second in which one can prevent the accident from being serious, can prevent the illness from entering in. One always has the choice. But it is for a fraction of a second and one must not miss it. If one misses it, it is finished.

One can make it afterwards? (laughter)

No. Afterwards there is yet another moment.... One has fallen, one is already hurt; but there is still a moment when one can change things for the better or worse, so that it may be something very fugitive the bad effects of which will quickly disappear or something which becomes as serious, as grave as it can be. I don't know if you have noticed that there are people who never miss the opportunity of an accident! Every time there is the possibility of an accident, they have it. And never is their accident ordinary. Every time the accident can be serious, it is serious. Well, usually in life one says: "Oh! he is unlucky, he is unfortunate, indeed he has no luck." But all that is ignorance. It depends absolutely on the working of his consciousness. I could give you examples — only I would have to speak about certain people and I don't want to. But I could give you striking examples! And this — this is the sort of thing one sees all the time, all the time here! There are people who could have been killed and who come out of it unscathed; there are others for whom it was not serious, and it becomes serious.

But that does not depend on thought, on the working of the ordinary thought. They may apparently have thoughts as good as the others — it is not that. It is the second of the choice — people knowing how to react just in the right way at the right time. I could give you hundreds of examples. It is quite interesting.

This depends absolutely on character. Some have such an awakened consciousness, so alert, that they are not asleep, they are awake within. Just at the second it is required they call the help. Or they invoke the divine Force. But just at the second it is needed. So the danger is averted, nothing happens. They could have been killed: they come out of it absolutely unhurt. Others, on the contrary, as soon as they have the least little scratch, something gets dislocated in their being: a sort of fright or pessimism or defeatism in their consciousness which automatically comes up — it was nothing, they had just twisted their leg and the next minute they break it. There is no reason for it. They could very well have not broken their leg.

There are others who climb up to a first floor on a ladder which gives way under them. They could have collapsed — they come out of that without the least hurt. How did they manage it? Apparently this seems wonderful, and still this is how things happen to them. They find themselves lying on the ground in an altogether fine state; nothing has happened to them. I could give you the names, I am telling you exact facts.

So, on what does this depend? It depends on whether one is sufficiently awake for the second of the choice to... And note that this is not at all mental, it is not that: it is an attitude of the being, it is the consciousness reacting in the right way. It goes quite far, very far, it is formidable, the power of this attitude. But as it is just a fraction of a second, it implies an altogether awakened consciousness which never sleeps, never enters the inconscient. For one does not know when these things are going to happen, isn't that so? Hence, one does not have the time to wake up. One must be awake.

I knew someone who, indeed, should have died and did not die because of this. For his consciousness reacted very fast. He had taken poison by mistake: instead of taking one dose of a certain medicine, he had taken twelve and it was a poison; he should have died, the heart should have stopped (it was many years ago) and he is still quite alive! He reacted in the right way.[51]   THE MOTHER

Remembering — Mantra from Within

It sometimes happens that when one is playing one does not remember the Divine, then suddenly one remembers and has the feeling that something breaks and one no longer plays well. Why?

Because everything is upset. That's the problem! So you think that when you are playing and do not remember, you play well! No, it is not quite that. It is that you do something with a certain concentration — work or play — and you are concentrated, but you have not developed the habit of mixing the remembrance of the Divine with the concentration (which is not difficult, but anyway, you do not have the habit) and then, suddenly the remembrance comes; then two things may happen: either the concentration is broken because you make an abrupt movement to seize the new attitude entering the consciousness, or else you feel a little remorse, a regret, a disquiet: "Oh! I did not remember"; that suffices, it upsets all you have done. For you change conditions completely. It is not the fact of remembering which makes you no longer play well, it is the fact of having disturbed your concentration. If you could remember without disturbing the concentration (which is not difficult), you would not only play well but would play better.

And then, you may also take another attitude. When you are playing and suddenly become aware that something is going wrong — you are making mistakes, are inattentive, sometimes opposing currents come across what you are doing — if you develop the habit, automatically at this moment, of calling as by a mantra, of repeating a word, that has an extraordinary effect. You choose your mantra; or rather, one day it comes to you spontaneously in a moment of difficulty. At a time when things are very difficult, when you have a sort of anguish, anxiety, when you don't know what is going to happen, suddenly this springs up in you, the word springs up in you. For each one it may be different. But if you mark this and each time you face a difficulty you repeat it, it becomes irresistible. For instance, if you feel you are about to fall ill, if you feel you are doing badly what you are doing, if you feel something evil is going to attack you, then.... But it must be a spontaneity in the being, it must spring up from you without your needing to think about it: you choose your mantra because it is a spontaneous expression of your aspiration; it may be one word, two or three words, a sentence, that depends on each one, but it must be a sound which awakens in you a certain condition. Then, when you have that, I assure you that you can pass through everything without difficulty. Even in the face of a real, veritable danger, an attack, for instance, by someone who wants to kill you, if, without getting excited, without being perturbed, you quietly repeat your mantra, one can do nothing to you. Naturally, you must truly be master of yourself; one part of the being must not be trembling there like a leaf; no, you must do it entirely, sincerely, then it is all-powerful. The best is when the word comes to you spontaneously: you call in a moment of great difficulty (mental, vital, physical, emotional, whatever it may be) and suddenly that springs up in you, two or three words, like magical words. You must remember these and form the habit of repeating them in moments when difficulties come. If you form the habit, one day it will come to you spontaneously: when the difficulty comes, at the same time the mantra will come. Then you will see that the results are wonderful. But it must not be an artificial thing or something you arbitrarily decide: "I shall use those words"; nor should somebody else tell you, "Oh! You know, this is very good" — it is perhaps very good for him but not for everyone.[52]   THE MOTHER

Listening to the Inner Law

The inner law, the truth of the being is the divine Presence in every human being, which should be the master and guide of our life.

When you acquire the habit of listening to this inner law, when you obey it, follow it, try more and more to let it guide your life, you create around you an atmosphere of truth and peace and harmony which naturally reacts upon circumstances and forms, so to say, the atmosphere in which you live. When you are a being of justice, truth, harmony, compassion, understanding, of perfect goodwill, this inner attitude, the more sincere and total it is, the more it reacts upon the external circumstances; not that it necessarily diminishes the difficulties of life, but it gives these difficulties a new meaning and that allows you to face them with a new strength and a new wisdom; whereas the man, the human being who follows his impulses, who obeys his desires, who has no time for scruples, who comes to live in complete cynicism, not caring for the effect that his life has upon others or for the more or less harmful consequences of his acts, creates for himself an atmosphere of ugliness, selfishness, conflict and bad will which necessarily acts more and more upon his consciousness and gives a bitterness to his life that in the end becomes a perpetual torment.

Of course this does not mean that such a man will not succeed in what he undertakes, that he will not be able to possess what he desires; these external advantages disappear only when there is within the inmost being a spark of sincerity which persists and makes him worthy of this misfortune.

If you see a bad man become unlucky and miserable,

you must immediately respect him. It means that the flame of inner sincerity is not altogether extinguished and something still reacts to his bad actions.[53]   THE MOTHER

8

YOGA-SHAKTI

There is a force which accompanies the growth of the new consciousness and at once grows with it and helps it to come about and to perfect itself. This force is the Yoga-Shakti. It is here coiled up and asleep in all the centres of our inner being (Chakras) and is at the base what is called in the Tantras the Kundalini Shakti. But it is also above us, above our head as the Divine Force — not there coiled up, involved, asleep, but awake, scient, potent, extended and wide; it is there waiting for manifestation and to this Force we have to open ourselves — to the power of the Mother. In the mind it manifests itself as a divine mind-force or a universal mind-force and it can do everything that the personal mind cannot do; it is then the yogic mind-force. When it manifests and acts in the vital or the physical in the same way, it is there apparent as a yogic life-force or a yogic body-force. It can awake in all these forms, bursting outwards and upwards, extending itself into wideness from below; or it can descend and become there a definite power for things; it can pour downwards into the body, working, establishing its reign, extending into wideness from above, link the lowest in us with the highest above us, release the individual into a cosmic universality or into absoluteness and transcendence.[54]

SRI AUROBINDO

There is a Yoga-Shakti lying coiled or asleep in the inner body, not active. When one does yoga, this force uncoils itself and rises upward to meet the Divine Consciousness and Force that are waiting above us. When this happens, when the awakened Yoga-Shakti arises, it is often felt like a snake uncoiling and standing up straight and lifting itself more and more upwards. When it meets the Divine Consciousness above, then the force of the Divine Consciousness can more easily descend into the body and be felt working there to change the nature.[55]

SRI AUROBINDO

... "There is a Yoga-Shakti lying coiled or asleep..."
How can it be awakened?

I think it awakens quite naturally the moment one takes the resolution to do the yoga. If the resolution is sincere and one has an aspiration, it wakes up by itself.

In fact, it is perhaps its awakening which gives the aspiration to do yoga.

It is possible that it is a result of the Grace... or after some conversation or reading, something that has suddenly given you the idea and aspiration to know what yoga is and to practise it. Sometimes just a simple conversation with someone is enough or a passage one reads from a book; well, it awakens this Yoga-Shakti and it is this which makes you do your yoga.

One is not aware of it at first — except that something has changed in our life, a new decision is taken, a turning.[56]

THE MOTHER

Something there is in us or something has to be developed, perhaps a central and still occult part of our being containing forces whose powers in our actual and present make-up are only a fraction of what could be, but if they became complete and dominant would be truly able to bring about with the help of the light and force of the soul and the supramental truth-consciousness the necessary physical transformation and its consequences. This might be found in the system of Chakras revealed by Tantric knowledge and accepted in the systems of Yoga, conscious centres and sources of all the dynamic powers of our being organising their action through the plexuses and arranged in an ascending series from the lowest physical to the highest mind centre and spiritual centre called the thousand-petalled lotus where ascending Nature, the Serpent Power of the Tantrics, meets the Brahman and is liberated into the Divine Being. These centres are closed or half closed within us and have to be opened before their full potentiality can be manifested in our physical nature: but once they are opened and completely active, no limit can easily be set to the development of their potencies and the total transformation to be possible.[57]   SRI AUROBINDO

9

ASPIRATION AND PRAYER

The efficacy of prayer is often doubted and prayer itself supposed to be a thing irrational and necessarily superfluous and ineffective. It is true that the universal will executes always its aim and cannot be deflected by egoistic propitiation and entreaty, it is true of the Transcendent who expresses himself in the universal order that, being omniscient, his larger knowledge must foresee the thing to be done and it does not need direction or stimulation by human thought and that the individual's desires are not and cannot be in any world-order the true determining factor. But neither is that order or the execution of the universal will altogether effected by mechanical Law, but by powers and forces of which for human life at least, human will, aspiration and faith are not among the least important. Prayer is only a particular form given to that will, aspiration and faith. Its forms are very often crude and not only childlike, which is in itself no defect, but childish; but still it has a real power and significance. Its power and sense is to put the will, aspiration and faith of man into touch with the divine Will as that of a conscious Being with whom we can enter into conscious and living relations. For our will and aspiration can act either by our own strength and endeavour, which can no doubt be made a thing great and effective whether for lower or higher purposes, — and there are plenty of disciplines which put it forward as the one force to be used, — or it can act in dependence upon and with subordination to the divine or the universal Will. And this latter way, again, may either look upon that Will as responsive indeed to our aspiration, but almost mechanically, by a sort of law of energy, or at any rate quite impersonally, or else it may look upon it as responding consciously to the divine aspiration and faith of the human soul and consciously bringing to it the help, the guidance, the protection and fruition demanded....[58]   SRI AUROBINDO

Do prayers and aspirations also take a form like thoughts?

Yes. At times they take even the form of the person who has the aspiration or makes the prayer — often. That depends. Aspirations sometimes take the form of that to which one aspires, but most often, and specially prayers, clearly take the form of the one who prays.

What is the difference between prayer and aspiration?

I have written this somewhere. There are several kinds of prayers.

There is the purely mechanical, material prayer, with words which have been learnt and are mechanically repeated. That does not signify anything much. And that has usually only one single result, that of quietening the person who prays, for if a prayer is repeated several times, the words end up by making you calm.

There is a prayer which is a spontaneous formula for expressing something precise which one wants to ask for: one prays for this thing or that, one prays for one thing or another; one can pray for somebody, for a circumstance, for oneself.

There is a point where aspiration and prayer meet, for there are prayers which are the spontaneous formulation of a lived experience: these spring up all ready from within the being, like something that's the expression of a profound experience, and which offers thanksgiving for that experience or asks its continuation or asks for its explanation also; and that indeed is quite close to aspiration. But aspiration is not necessarily formulated in words; or if it is formulated in words, it is almost a movement of invocation. You aspire for a certain state; for instance, you have found something in yourself that is not in keeping with your ideal, a movement of darkness and ignorance, perhaps even of ill-will, something that's not in harmony with what you want to realise; then that is not going to be formulated in words; that will be like a springing flame and like an offering made of a living experience, asking to grow larger, be magnified and ever more and more clear and precise. All that may be put into words *later*, if one tries to remember and note down one's experience. But aspiration always springs up like a flame that rises high and carries in itself the thing one desires to be or what one desires to do or desires to have. I use the word "desire", but truly it is here that the word "aspire" should be used, for that does not have either the quality or the form of a desire.

It is truly like a great purifying flame of will, and it carries in its core the thing that asks to be realised.

For instance, if you have done something you regret having done, if that has unhappy consequences which disturb things, and several people are implicated, you do not know the reactions of the others, but you yourself wish that what has been done may take a turn for the best, and that if there is a mistake, it may be understood, and that no matter what the mistake, this may be for you an opportunity for a greater progress, a greater discipline, a new ascent towards the Divine, a door open on a future that you want to be more clear and true and intense; so all this is gathered here (*pointing to the heart*) like a force, and then it surges up and rises in a great movement of ascent, and at times without the shadow of a formulation, without words, without expression, but like a springing flame.

That indeed is true aspiration. That may happen a hundred, a thousand times daily if one is in that state in which one constantly wants to progress and be more true and more fully in harmony with what the Divine Will wants of us.

Prayer is a much more external thing, generally about a precise fact, and always formulated for it is the formula that makes the prayer. One may have an aspiration and transcribe it as a prayer, but aspiration goes beyond prayer in every way. It is much closer and much more as it were self-forgetful, living only in the thing one wants to be or do, and the offering of all that one wants to do to the Divine. You may pray in order to ask for something, you may also pray to thank the Divine for what He has given you, and that prayer is much greater: it may be called an act of thanksgiving. You may pray in gratitude for the aspect of kindness the Divine has shown to you, for what He has done for you, for what you see in Him, and the praise you want to offer Him. And all this may take the form of a prayer. It is decidedly the highest prayer, for it is not exclusively preoccupied with oneself, it is not an egoistic prayer.

Certainly, one may have an aspiration in all the domains, but the very centre of aspiration is in the psychic being, whilst one may pray in all the domains, and the prayer belongs to the domain in which one prays. One may make purely material, physical prayers, vital prayers, mental prayers, psy-chic prayers, spiritual prayers, and each one has its special character, its special value.

There is a kind of prayer at once spontaneous and un-selfish which is like a great call, usually not for one's own self personally, but like something that may be called an inter-cession with the Divine. It is extremely powerful. I have had countless instances of things which have been realised almost instantaneously due to prayers of this kind. It implies a great faith, a great ardour, a great sincerity, and a great simplicity of heart also, something that does not calculate, does not plan, does not bargain, does not give with the idea of receiving in exchange. For, the majority of men give with one hand and hold out the other to get something in exchange; the largest number of prayers are of that sort. But there are others of the kind I have described, acts of thanksgiving, a kind of canticle, and these are very good.

There you are. I don't know if I have made myself clear, but this is how it is.

To be clearer, we may say that prayer is always for-mulated in words; but the words may have different values according to the state in which they are formulated. Prayer is a formulated thing and one may aspire. But it is difficult to pray without praying to someone. For instance, those who have a conception of the universe from which they have more or less driven out the idea of the Divine (there are many people of this kind; this idea troubles them — the idea that there is someone who knows all, can do everything and who is so formidably greater than they that there can be no comparison; that's a bit troublesome for their *amour-propre*; so they try to make a world without the Divine), these people evidently cannot pray, for to whom would they pray? Unless they pray to themselves, which is not the custom! But one can aspire for something without having any faith in the Divine. There are people who do not believe in the existence of a God, but who have faith in progress. They have the idea that the world is in constant progress and that this progress will go on indefinitely without stopping, towards an ever greater betterment. Well, these people can have a very great aspiration for progress, and they don't even need any idea of a divine existence for that. Aspiration necessarily implies a faith but not necessarily faith in a divine being; whilst prayer cannot exist if it is not addressed to a divine being. And pray to what? One does not pray to something that has no personality! One prays to someone who can hear us. If there is nobody to hear us, how could one pray? Hence, if one prays, this means that, even when one doesn't acknowledge it, one has faith in somebody infinitely higher than us, infinitely more powerful, who can change our destiny and change us also, if one prays so as to be heard. That is the essential difference.

So the more intellectual people admit aspiration and say that prayer is something inferior. The mystics tell you that aspiration is all very well but if you want to be really heard and want the Divine to listen to you, you must pray, and pray with the simplicity of a child, a perfect candour, that is, a perfect trust: "I need this or that (whether it be a moral need or a physical or material need), well, I ask You for it, give it to me." Or else: "You have given me what I asked of You, You have made me realise concretely those experiences which were unknown to me and are now marvels I can attain at will; yes, I am infinitely grateful to You and I offer a prayer of thanksgiving to sing Your praise and thank You for Your intervention." It is like that. To aspire it is not necessary to direct the aspiration to someone, towards someone. One has an aspiration for a certain state of being, for knowledge, for a realisation, a state of consciousness; one aspires for something, but it is not necessarily a prayer; prayer is something additional.

Prayer is a personal thing, addressed to a personal being, that is, to something — a force or a being — who can hear you and answer you. Otherwise you can't ask for anything.[59]

THE MOTHER

Aspiration is like an arrow, like this (*gesture*). So you aspire, want *very* earnestly to understand, know, enter into the truth. Yes? And then with that aspiration you do this (*gesture*). Your aspiration rises, rises, rises, rises straight up, very strong and then it strikes against a kind of... how to put it? ... lid which is there, hard like iron and extremely thick, and it does not pass through. And then you say, "See, what's the use of aspiring? It brings nothing at all. I meet with something hard and cannot pass!" But you know about the drop of water which falls on the rock, it ends up by making a chasm: it cuts the rock from top to bottom. Your aspiration is a drop of water which, instead of falling, rises. So, by dint of rising, it beats, beats, beats, and one day it makes a hole, by dint of rising; and when it makes the hole suddenly it springs out from this lid and enters an immensity of light, and you say, "Ah, now I understand."

It's like that.

So one must be very persistent, very stubborn and have an aspiration which rises straight upwards, that is, which does not go roaming around here and there, seeking all kinds of things.

Only this: to understand, understand, understand, to learn to know, to be.

When one reaches the very top, there is nothing more to understand, nothing more to learn, one *is*, and it's when one *is* that one understands and knows.[60]   THE MOTHER

Power of Spontaneous Aspiration

Mother, when we make an effort, there's something in us which becomes very self-satisfied and boastful and contented with this effort, and that spoils everything. Then how can we get rid of this?

Ah, that's what looks on at what it is doing! There is always someone who observes when one is doing something. Now sometimes, he becomes proud. Obviously, this takes away much strength from the effort. I think it is that: it is the habit of looking at oneself acting, looking at oneself living. It is necessary to observe oneself but I think it is still more necessary to try to be absolutely sincere and spontaneous, very spontaneous in what one does: not always to go on observing oneself, looking at what one is doing, judging oneself — sometimes severely. In fact it is almost as bad as patting oneself with satisfaction, the two are equally bad. One should be so sincere in his aspiration that he doesn't even know he is aspiring, that he becomes the aspiration itself. When this indeed can be realised, one truly attains to an extraordinary power.

One minute, one minute of this, and you can prepare years of realisation. When one is no longer a self-regarding being, an ego looking at itself acting, when one becomes the action itself, above all in the aspiration, this truly is good. When there is no longer a person who is aspiring, when it is an aspiration which leaps up with a fully concentrated impulsion, then truly it goes very far. Otherwise there is always mixed up in it a little vanity, a little self-complacency, a little self-pity also, all kinds of little things which come and spoil everything. But it is difficult.[61]   THE MOTHER

OBTAINING ANSWERS AND SOLUTIONS

*Once or twice, as a game, you took one of your books
or Sri Aurobindo's and opened a page at random, and
read out a sentence. Can these sentences give one a
sign or an indication? What should we do to get a
true answer?*

Everybody can do it. It is done in this way: you concentrate.
Now, it depends on what you want. If you have an inner problem and want the solution, you concentrate on this problem;
if you want to know the condition you are in, which you are
not aware of — if you want to get some light on the state you
are in, you just come forward with simplicity and ask for the
light. Or else, quite simply, if you are curious to know what
the invisible knowledge has to tell you, you remain silent and
still for a moment and then open the book. I always used to
recommend taking a paper-knife, because it is thinner; while
you are concentrated you insert it in the book and with the tip
indicate something. Then, if you know how to concentrate,
that is to say, if you really do it with an aspiration to have an
answer, it always comes.

For, in books of this kind (*Mother shows* The Synthesis
of Yoga), books of revelation, there is always an accumulation
of forces — at least of higher mental forces, and most often
of spiritual forces of the highest knowledge. Every book, on
account of the words it contains, is like a small accumulator of
these forces. People don't know this, for they don't know how

to make use of it, but it is so. In the same way, in every picture, photograph, there is an accumulation, a small accumulation representative of the force of the person whose picture it is, of his nature and, if he has powers, of his powers. Now, you, when you are sincere and have an aspiration, you emanate a certain vibration, the vibration of your aspiration which goes and meets the corresponding force in the book, and it is a higher consciousness which gives you the answer.

Everything is contained potentially. Each element of a whole potentially contains what is in the whole. It is a little difficult to explain, but you will understand with an example: when people want to practise magic, if they have a bit of nail or hair, it is enough for them, because within this, potentially, there is all that is in the being itself. And in a book there is potentially — not expressed, not manifest — the knowledge which is in the person who wrote the book. Thus, Sri Aurobindo represented a totality of comprehension and knowledge and power; and every one of his books is at once a symbol and a representation. Every one of his books contains symbolically, potentially, what is in him. Therefore, if you concentrate on the book, you can, through the book, go back to the source. And even, by passing through the book, you will be able to receive much more than what is just in the book.

There is always a way of reading and understanding what one reads, which gives an answer to what you want. It is not just a chance or an amusement, nor is it a kind of diversion. You may do it just "like that", and then nothing at all happens to you, you have no reply and it is not interesting. But if you do it seriously, if seriously your aspiration tries to concentrate on this instrument — it is like a battery, isn't it, which contains energies — if it tries to come into contact with the energy which is there and insists on having the answer to what it wants to know, well, naturally, the energy which is there — the union of the two forces, the force given out by you and that accumulated in the book — will guide your hand and your paper-knife or whatever you have; it will guide you exactly to the thing that expresses what you ought to know.... Obviously, if one does it without sincerity or conviction, nothing at all happens. If it is done sincerely, one gets an answer.

Certain books are like this, more powerfully charged than others; there are others where the result is less clear. But generally, books containing aphorisms and short sentences — not very long philosophical explanations, but rather things in a condensed and precise form — it is with these that one succeeds best.

Naturally, the value of the answer depends on the value of the spiritual force contained in the book. If you take a novel, it will tell you nothing at all but stupidities. But if you take a book containing a condensation of forces — of knowledge or spiritual force or teaching power — you will receive your answer.[62]   THE MOTHER

The noise made by all the words, all the ideas in your head is so deafening that it prevents you from hearing the truth when it wants to manifest.

To learn to be quiet and silent... When you have a problem to solve, instead of turning over in your head all the possibilities, all the consequences, all the possible things one should or should not do, if you remain quiet with an aspiration for goodwill, if possible a need for goodwill, the solution comes very quickly. And as you are silent you are able to hear it.

When you are caught in a difficulty, try this method: instead of becoming agitated, turning over all the ideas and actively seeking solutions, of worrying, fretting, running here and there inside your head — I don't mean externally, for externally you probably have enough common sense not to do that! but inside, in your head — *remain quiet*. And according to your nature, with ardour or peace, with intensity or widening or with all these together, implore the Light and wait for it to come.

In this way the path would be considerably shortened.[63]

THE MOTHER

11

POWER OF CONTROL

Self-Control

There is always a moment when everyone has self-control.
And if one had not said "Yes" once, if one had not taken the
decision, one would not have done it.

There is not one human being who has not the energy
and capacity to resist something imposed upon him — if he is
left free to do so. People tell you, "I can't do otherwise" — it
is because in the depths of their heart they *do not want* to do
otherwise; they have accepted to be the slaves of their vice.
There is a moment when one accepts.[64]   THE MOTHER

Controlling Others — Power of Mastery

One can't control outer matter if one does not control inner
matter, for they are the same thing.

... mastery means the knowledge of handling certain
vibrations; if you know how to handle these vibrations
you have the mastery. The best field of experimentation
is yourself: first you have the control in yourself and once
you have it in yourself you can transmit the vibration to
others, to the extent you are capable of identifying yourself
with them and of thus creating this vibration in them. And
if you cannot handle a vibration in yourself, you don't even

know the procedure; you don't even know what to do, so how can you manipulate it in others? You may encourage them by words, by an influence over them, to do what is needed to learn self-control, but you cannot control them directly.

To control something, a movement, is simply to replace by one's presence, without words or explanations, the bad vibration by the true one. This is what constitutes the power of mastery. It does not lie in speaking, in explaining; with words and explanations and even a certain emanation of force, you may have an influence on someone, but you do not control his movement. The control of the movement is the capacity to oppose the vibration of this movement by a stronger, truer vibration which can stop the other one... I could give you an example, you know, a very easy one. Two people are arguing in front of you; not only are they arguing, but they are on the point of coming to blows; so you explain to them that this is not the thing to do, you give them good reasons for stopping and they come to a stop. You will have had an influence on them. But if you simply stand before them and look at them and send out a vibration of peace, calm, quietude, without saying a word, without any explanation, the other vibration will no longer be able to last, it will fall away of itself. That is mastery.

The same thing applies to the cure of ignorance. If you need words to explain something, that is not true knowledge. If I have to say all that I do say for you to understand me, that is not mastery, it is simply that I am able to exercise an influence on your intelligence and help you to understand and awaken in you the desire to know and discipline yourselves, etc. But if by looking at you, without saying anything I am not able to make the light enter into you, the light which will make you understand, I won't have mastered the movement or the state of ignorance.[65] THE MOTHER

12

POWER OF IMMOBILITY

*Sweet Mother, I don't understand "the strong im-
mobility of an immortal spirit* (Sri Aurobindo, *The
Synthesis of Yoga)".*

What is it you don't understand? That an immortal spirit has a
strong immobility? It says what it means. An immortal spirit is
necessarily immobile and strong, by the very fact of its being
immortal....

For this is a fact, it's like that. When the spirit is conscious of immortality, it becomes an immobility all made
of strength. Immobility — that is to say, it doesn't move any
longer, but it is a strong immobility, it is not an immobility
of inertia or impotence; it is a strong immobility which is
a basis for action, that is, all one does founds itself upon
this powerful — all-powerful — immobility of the spirit that
is immortal.

But you see, there is no explanation which can give you
that; you must have the experience, one can't understand what
this means.... And it is the same for everything: the head,
the little brain, cannot understand. The minute one has the
experience, one understands — not before. One may have a
sort of imaginative idea, but this is not understanding. To understand one must live it. When you become conscious of your
immortal spirit, you will know what its strong immobility is
— but not before. Otherwise, these are mere words.

You don't understand how one can be immobile and strong at the same time, is that what is bothering you? Well, I reply that the greatest strength is in immobility. That is the sovereign power.

And there is a very small superficial application of this which perhaps you will understand. Someone comes and insults you or says unpleasant things to you; and if you begin to vibrate in unison with this anger or this ill-will, you feel quite weak and powerless and usually you make a fool of yourself. But if you manage to keep within yourself, especially in your head, a complete immobility which refuses to receive these vibrations, then at the same time you feel a great strength, and the other person cannot disturb you. If you remain very quiet, even physically, and when violence is directed at you, you are able to remain very quiet, very silent, very still, well, that has a power not only over you but over the other person also. If you don't have all these vibrations of inner response, if you can remain absolutely immobile within yourself, everywhere, this has an almost immediate effect upon the other person.

That gives you an idea of the power of immobility. And it is a very common fact which can occur every day; it is not a great event of spiritual life, it is something of the outer, material life.

There is a tremendous power in immobility: mental immobility, sensorial immobility, physical immobility. If you can remain like a wall, absolutely motionless, everything the other person sends you will immediately fall back upon him. And it has an immediate action. It can stop the arm of the assassin, you understand, it has that strength. Only, one must not just appear to be immobile and yet be boiling inside! That's not what I mean. I mean an integral immobility.[66]   THE MOTHER

... there is a static power. How to explain it to you? Look, there is the same difference between static power and dynamic power as between a game of defence and a game of attack; you understand? It is the same thing. Static power is something which can withstand everything, nothing can act upon it, nothing can touch it, nothing can shake it — it is immobile, but it is invincible. Dynamic power is something in action, which at times goes forth and may at times receive blows. That is to say, if you want your dynamic power to be always victorious, it must be supported by a considerable static power, an unshakable base.

I know what you want to say... that a human being becomes aware of power only when it is dynamic; a human being doesn't consider it a power except when it acts; if it doesn't act he does not even notice it, he does not realise the tremendous force which is behind this inaction — at times, even frequently, a force more formidable than the power which acts. But you may try it out in yourself, you will see, it is much more difficult to remain calm, immobile, unshakable before something very unpleasant — whether it be words or acts levelled against you — infinitely more difficult than to answer with the same violence. Suppose someone insults you; if in the face of these insults, you can remain immobile (not only outwardly, I mean integrally), without being shaken or touched in any way: you are there like a force against which one can do nothing and you do not reply, you do not make a gesture, you do not say a word, all the insults thrown at you leave you absolutely untouched, within and without; you can keep your heart-beats absolutely quiet, you can keep the thoughts in your head quite immobile and calm without their being in the least disturbed, that is, your head does not answer immediately by similar vibrations and your nerves don't feel clenched with the need to return a few blows to relieve themselves; if you can be like that, you have a static power, and it is infinitely more powerful than if you had that kind of force which makes you answer insult by insult, blow by blow and agitation by agitation.[67]   THE MOTHER

... some people are more or less what I call "coddled", that is, unable to resist any pain, to bear it; they immediately say, "I can't! It is unbearable. I can't bear any more!" Ah, this indeed changes nothing in the circumstances; it does not stop the suffering, because it is not by telling it that you don't want it that you make it go away. But if one can do two things: either bring into oneself — for all nervous suffering, for example — bring into oneself a kind of immobility, as total as possible, at the place of pain, this has the effect of an anaesthetic. If one succeeds in bringing an inner immobility, an immobility of the inner vibration, at the spot where one is suffering, it has exactly the same effect as an anaesthetic. It cuts off the contact between the place of pain and the brain, and once you have cut the contact, if you can keep this state long enough, the pain will disappear. You must form the habit of doing this. But you have the occasion, all the time, the opportunity to do it: you get a cut, get a knock, you see, one always gets a little hurt somewhere — especially when doing athletics, gymnastics and all that — well, these are opportunities given to us. Instead of sitting there observing the pain, trying to analyse it, concentrating upon it, which makes it increase indefinitely... There are people who think of something else but it does not last; they think of something else and then suddenly are drawn back to the place that hurts. But if one can do this... You see, since the pain is there, it proves that you are in contact with the nerve that's transmitting the pain, otherwise you wouldn't feel it. Well, once you know that you are in contact, you try to accumulate at that point as much immobility as you can, to stop the vibration of the pain; you will perceive then that it has the effect of a limb which goes to sleep when you are in an awkward position and that all of a sudden... you know, don't you?... and then, when it stops, it begins to vibrate again terribly. Well, you deliberately try this kind of concentration of immobility in the painful nerve; at the painful point you bring as total an immobility as you can. Well, you will see that it works, as I told you, like an anaesthetic: it puts the thing to sleep. And then, if you can add to that a kind of inner peace and a trust that the pain will go away, well, I tell you that it will go.

Of all things, that which is considered the most difficult from the yogic point of view is toothache, because it is very close to the brain. Well, I know that this can be done truly to the extent of not feeling the pain at all; and this does not cure the bad tooth, but there are cases in which one can succeed in killing the painful nerve. Usually in a tooth it is the nerve which has been attacked by the caries, the disease, and which begins to protest with all its strength. So, if you succeed in establishing this immobility, you prevent it from vibrating, you prevent it from protesting. And what is remarkable is that if you do it fairly constantly, with sufficient perseverance, the sick nerve will die and you will not suffer at all any more. Because it was that which was suffering and when it is dead it does not suffer any longer. Try.[68]   THE MOTHER

13

POWER OF IDENTIFICATION

One can learn how to identify oneself. One must learn. It is indispensable if one wants to get out of one's ego. For so long as one is shut up in one's ego, one can't make any progress.

How can it be done?

There are many processes. I'll tell you one.

When I was in Paris, I used to go to many places where there were gatherings of all kinds, people making all sorts of researches, spiritual (so-called spiritual), occult researches, etc. And once I was invited to meet a young lady (I believe she was Swedish) who had found a process of knowledge, exactly a process for learning. And so she explained it to us. We were three or four (her French was not very good but she was quite sure of herself!); she said: "It's like this, you take an object or make a sign on a blackboard or take a drawing — that is not important — take whatever is most convenient for you. Suppose, for instance, that I draw for you... (she had a blackboard) I draw a design." She drew a kind of half-geometric design. "Now, you sit in front of the design and concentrate all your attention upon it — upon that design which is there. You concentrate, concentrate without letting anything else enter your consciousness — except that. Your eyes are fixed on the drawing and don't move at all. You are as it were hypnotised by the drawing. You look (and so she sat there, looking), you look, look, look.... I don't know, it takes more or less time, but still for one who is used to it, it goes pretty fast. You look, look, look, you *become* that drawing you are looking at. Nothing else exists in the world any longer except the drawing, and then, suddenly, you pass to the other side; and when you pass to the other side you enter a new consciousness, and you know."

We had a good laugh, for it was amusing. But it is quite true, it is an excellent method to practise. Naturally, instead of taking a drawing or any object, you may take, for instance, an idea, a few words. You have a problem preoccupying you, you don't know the solution of the problem; well, you objectify your problem in your mind, put it in the most precise, exact, succinct terms possible, and then concentrate, make an effort; you concentrate only on the words, and if possible on the idea they represent, that is, upon your problem — you concentrate, concentrate, concentrate until nothing else exists but that. And it is true that, all of a sudden, you have the feeling of something opening, and one is on the other side. The other side of what?... It means that you have opened a door of your consciousness, and instantaneously you have the solution of your problem.

It is an excellent method of learning "how" to identify oneself.

For instance, you are with someone. This person tells you something, you tell him the contrary (as it usually happens, simply through a spirit of contradiction) and you begin arguing. Naturally, you will never come to any point, except a quarrel if you are ill-natured. But instead of doing that, instead of remaining in your own ideas or your own words, if you tell yourself: "Wait a little, I am going to try and see why he said that to me. Yes, why did he tell me that?" And you concentrate: "Why, why, why?" You stand there, just like that, trying. The other person continues speaking, doesn't he? — and is very happy too, for you don't contradict him any longer! He talks profusely and is sure he has convinced you. Then you concentrate more and more on what he is saying, and with the feeling that gradually, through his words, you are entering his mind. When you enter his head, suddenly you enter into his way of thinking, and next, just imagine, you understand why he is speaking to you thus! And then, if you have a fairly swift intelligence and put what you have just come to understand alongside what you had known before, you have the two ways together, and so can find the truth reconciling both. And here you have truly made progress. And this is the best way of widening one's thought.

If you are beginning an argument, keep quiet immediately, instantaneously. You must be silent, say nothing at all, and then try to see the thing as the other person sees it — that won't make you forget your own way of seeing it, not at all! but you will be able to put both of them together. And you will truly have made progress, a real progress.

It is the same for everything. In all that you do together with others, if you do not agree, take it as a divine Grace, a marvellous opportunity given you to make a progress. And it is simple: instead of being on this side, you are on the other; instead of looking at yourself, you enter the other person and look. You must have just a little bit of imagination, a little more control over your thoughts, over your movements. But that is not very difficult. When you have tried it out a little, after a while you find it very easy.

You must not just look and then make a mental effort, telling yourself: "Why is it like this and like that? Why does he do that? Why does he say that?" You will never arrive at anything. You won't understand, you will imagine all kinds of explanations which will be worthless and teach you nothing at all except to tell yourself: "That person is stupid or else wicked" — things that lead nowhere. On the other hand, if you only make that little movement, and instead of looking at him as an object quite alien to you, you try to enter within, you enter within, into that little head that's before you, and then, suddenly, you find yourself on the other side, you look at yourself and understand quite well what he is saying — everything is clear, the why, the how, the reason, the feeling which is behind the whole thing.... It is an experiment you have the opportunity of making a hundred times a day.

At first you won't succeed very well, but if you persist, you will end up by succeeding admirably. This adds a lot of interest to life. And besides it is a work which really makes you progress, for it makes you come out of that little armour of yours in which you are nicely shut up, in which you knock against everything. You have seen moths knocking against the light, haven't you?... Everyone's consciousness is like that, it goes along knocking here, knocking there, for these are things foreign to it. But instead of knocking about, one enters within, then it begins to become a part of oneself. One widens oneself, breathes freely, has enough space to move in, one doesn't knock against anything, one enters, penetrates, understands. And one lives in many places at the same time. It is very interesting, one does it automatically.

For instance, when you are reading a book that interests you very much, a wonderful novel full of exciting adventures, when you are completely absorbed in the story, at times you forget your class-hour or even dinner-time or your bed-time.

You are completely absorbed in what you are reading. Well, this is a phenomenon of self-identification. And if you do it with a certain perfection, you succeed in understanding ahead what is going to happen. There is a moment when, being fully absorbed in the story, you come to know (without trying to look for it) towards what end the author is leading you, how he is going to unfold his story and come to his conclusion. For you have identified yourself with the creative thought of the author. You do it more or less perfectly, without knowing that you are doing it, but these are phenomena of self-identification.

There are, in Paris, theatres of the third or fourth rank where sensational dramas are performed. These are suburban theatres. They are not for intellectuals but for the masses, and all the elements are always extremely dramatic, moving. Well, those who go there are mostly very simple people and forget completely that they are in a theatre. They identify themselves with the drama. And so, things like this happen: on the stage there is the traitor hiding behind the door, and the hero comes along, not aware naturally that the traitor is hiding there and he is going to be killed. Now, there are people sitting up there (in what is called the gallery), right up in the theatre, who shout: "Look out, he is there!" (*Laughter*) It has not happened just once, it happens hundreds of times, spontaneously. I had seen a play of this kind called *Le Bossu*, I believe; anyway it was quite a sensational drama and it was being played at the *Théâtre de la Porte Saint-Martin*. In this play there was a room. On the stage a large room could be seen and at its side a small room and... I don't remember the story now, but in the small room there was a button which could be pressed, and by pressing the button the ceiling of the bigger room could be brought down on those who were there so as to crush them inexorably!... And a warning had been given, people had already spoken about it, passed on the word. And now there was a traitor who had hidden himself in the little room and he knew the trick of the button, and then there was the hero who came in with other people, and they started arguing; and everyone knew that the ceiling was going to come down.... I didn't say anything, I remembered I was in the theatre, I was waiting to see how the author was going to get out of this situation to save his hero (for it was evident he couldn't kill him off like that before everybody!). But the others were not at all in the same state. Well, there were spectators who shouted, really shouted: "Look out, mind the ceiling!" That's how it was.

These are phenomena of self-identification. Only, they are involuntary. And this is also one of the methods used today to cure nervous diseases. When someone cannot sleep, cannot be restful because he is too excited and nervous and his nerves are ill and weakened by excessive agitation, he is told to sit in front of an aquarium, for instance — an aquarium, that's very lovely, isn't it? — before an aquarium with pretty little fish in it, goldfish; just to sit there, settle down in an easy-chair and try not to think of anything (particularly not of his troubles) and look at the fish. So he looks at the fish, moving around, coming and going, swimming, gliding, turning, meeting, crossing, chasing one another indefinitely, and also the water flowing slowly and the passing fish. After a while he lives the life of fishes: he comes and goes, swims, glides, plays. And at the end of the hour his nerves are in a perfect state and he is completely restful!

But the condition is that one must not think of one's troubles, simply watch the fish.

Can the Divine be attained in this way?

Do you understand, the only way of knowing the Divine is by identifying oneself with Him. There is no other, there is only one, one single way. Hence, once you are master of this method of identification, you can identify yourself. So you choose your object for identification, you want to identify yourself with the Divine. But so long as you do not know how to identify yourself, a hundred and one things will always come across your path, pulling you here, pulling you there, scattering you, and you will not be able to identify yourself with Him. But if you have learnt how to identify yourself, then you have only to orientate the identification, place it where you want it, and then hold on there until you get a result. It will come very fast if you are master of your power of identification. Yes, it will come very quickly. Ramakrishna used to say that the time could vary between three days, three hours and three minutes. Three days for very slow people, three hours for those who were a little swifter, three minutes for those who are used to it.[69]   THE MOTHER

Widening One's Identification

Why do human beings always want to have some-thing in exchange for what they give?

Because they are shut up in themselves.

They sense their limitation and think that in order to grow, increase and even survive, they need to take things from outside, for they live in the consciousness of their personal limitation. So, for them, what they give makes a hole and this hole must be filled up by receiving something!... Naturally, this is a mistake. And the truth is that if instead of being shut up in the narrow limits of their little person, they could so widen their consciousness as to be able not only to identify themselves with others in their narrow limits, but to come out of these limits, pass beyond, spread out everywhere, unite with the one Consciousness and become all things, then, at that moment the narrow limits will vanish, but not before. And as long as one senses the narrow limits, one wants to take, for one fears to lose. One spends and wants to replenish. It is due to that, my child. For if one were spread out in all things, if all the vibrations which come and go expressed the need to merge into everything, to widen oneself, grow, not by remaining within one's limits but coming out of them, and finally to be identified with everything, one would no longer have anything to lose for one would have everything. Only, one doesn't know this. And so, as one doesn't know, one can't do it. One tries to take, accumulate, accumulate, accumulate, but that is impossible, one can't accumulate. One must identify oneself. And then, the little bit one gives, one wants to get back: one gives a good thought, one expects some recognition; one gives a little affection, one expects it from others... for one doesn't have the ability to become the good thought in everything, one doesn't have the ability to be the affection, the tender love in all things. One feels just like that, all cut up and limited, and fears to lose everything, fears to lose what one has because one would be impoverished. On the other hand, if one were able to identify oneself, one would no longer need to pull. The more one spreads out, the more one has. The more one gets identified, the more one becomes. And then, instead of taking, one gives. And the more one gives, the more one grows.

But for this, one must be able to come out of the limits of one's little ego. One must be identified with the Force, identified with the Vibration instead of being identified with one's ego.

It is very difficult, but one can succeed.[70]

THE MOTHER

14

POWER OVER ILLNESS AND PAIN

Illnesses enter through the subtle body, don't they?
How can they be stopped?

Ah! Here we are.... If one is very sensitive, very sensitive
— one must be very sensitive — the moment they touch the
subtle body and try to pass through, one feels it. It is not like
something touching the body, it is a sort of feeling. If you are
able to perceive it at that moment, you have still the power
to say "no", and it goes away. But for this one must be extremely sensitive. However, that develops. All these things can
be developed methodically by the will. You can become quite
conscious of this envelope, and if you develop it sufficiently,
you don't even need to look and see, you feel that something
has touched you. I can give you an instance of this, there are
many similar ones.

Someone was seeking to establish a constant and conscious contact — absolutely constant and conscious — with
the inner Godhead, not only with the psychic being but the
divine Presence in the psychic being, and she had decided
that she would be like this, that she would busy herself with
nothing else, that is to say, whatever she might be doing,
her concentration was upon this, and even when she went
out walking in the street, her concentration was upon this.
She lived in a big city where there was much traffic: buses,
tramways, etc., many things, and to cross the street one had to
be considerably careful, wide-awake and attentive, otherwise

one could get run over, but this person had resolved that she would not come out of her concentration. One day when she was crossing one of the big avenues with all its cars and its tramways, still deep in her concentration, in her inner seeking, she suddenly felt at about an arm's length a little shock, like this; she jumped back and a car passed just by her side. If she had not jumped back she would have been run over.... This is an extreme point, but without going so far one can very easily feel a kind of little discomfort (it is not something which is imposed with a great force), a little uneasiness coming near you from anywhere at all: front, behind, above, below. If at that moment you are sufficiently alert, you say "no", as though you were cutting off the contact with great strength, and it is finished. If you are not conscious at that moment, the next minute or a few minutes later you get a queer sick feeling inside, a cold in the back, a little uneasiness, the beginning of some disharmony; you feel a maladjustment somewhere, as though the general harmony had been disturbed. Then you must concentrate all the more and with a great strength of will keep the faith that nothing can do you harm, nothing can touch you. This suffices, you can throw off the illness at that moment. But you must do this immediately, you understand, you must not wait five minutes, it must be done at once. If you wait too long and begin to feel really an uneasiness somewhere, and something begins to get quite disturbed, then it is good to sit down, concentrate and call the Force, concentrate it on the place which is getting disturbed, that is to say, which is beginning to become ill. But if you don't do anything at all, an illness indeed gets lodged somewhere; and all this, because you were not sufficiently alert. And sometimes one is obliged to follow the entire curve to find the favourable moment again and get rid of the business. I have said somewhere that in the physical domain all is a question of method — a method is necessary for realising everything. And if the illness has succeeded in touching the physical-physical, well, you must follow the procedure needed to get rid of it. This is what medical science calls "the course of the illness". One can hasten the course with the help of spiritual forces, but all the same the procedure must be followed. There are some four different stages. The very first is instantaneous. The second can be done in some minutes, the third may take several hours and the fourth several days. And then, once the thing is lodged there, all will depend not only on the receptivity of the body but still more on the willingness of the part which is the cause of the disorder. You know, when the thing comes from outside it is in affinity with something inside. If it manages to pass through, to enter without one's being aware of it, it means there is some affinity somewhere, and the part of the being which has responded must be convinced.

I have known some truly extraordinary instances. If you can at the moment... Wait, take an example which is quite concrete: sunstroke. This upsets you considerably, it is one of the things which makes you most ill — a sunstroke upsets everything, it disturbs the inner functions, it generally causes a congestion in the head and very high fever. So, if this has happened, if it has succeeded in getting through the protection and entering you, well, if you can just go into a quiet place, stretch yourself out flat, go out of your body (naturally, you must learn this; there are people who do this spontaneously, for others a long discipline is necessary), go out of your body, remain above in a way to be able to see the body (you know the phenomenon, seeing one's body when one is outside? This

can be done at will, going out of one's body and remaining
just above it), the body is stretched out on a bed, a bench,
on the ground, anywhere; you are stretched just above it and
from there, consciously, you pull the Force from above, and
if you are used to doing it, if your aspiration is strong enough,
you get the answer; and then, from there, taking care not to
re-enter your body, you begin to push these forces into the
body, like that, regularly, until you see the body receiving
them (for, the first few moments they don't enter, because
the body is quite upset by the illness, it is not receptive, it
is curled up), you push them gently, gently, quietly, without
nervousness, very peacefully, into the body. But you must not
be disturbed by anyone. If someone comes along, sees you
stretched out and shakes you, it is extremely dangerous. You
must do this in quiet conditions, ask people not to disturb you
or better shut yourself up where they can't disturb you. But
you can concentrate slowly (this takes more or less time —
ten minutes, half an hour, one hour, two hours — it depends
upon the seriousness of the disorder which has set in), slowly,
from above, you concentrate the Force until you see that the
body is receiving, that the Force is entering, the disorder is
being set right and there is a relaxation in the body itself.
Once that is done you can get back and you are cured. This
has been done for a sunstroke, which is a fairly violent thing,
and also for typhoid fever, and many other illnesses, as, for
instance, for a liver which was suddenly upset somehow (not
due to indigestion, but a liver which doesn't function properly
for the moment); it may also be cured in the same way. There
was a case of cholera which was healed like that. The cholera
had just been caught, had entered, but was not yet lodged; it
was completely cured. Consequently, when I say that if one

masters the spiritual force and knows how to use it, there is no malady which cannot be cured, I don't say it just like that in the air; it is said from experience with the thing. Of course, you will say you don't know how to go out of the body, draw the Force, concentrate it, have all this mastery.... It is not very frequent, but it is not impossible. And one can be sure that if one is helped... In fact, there is a much easier method, it is to call for help.

But the condition in every case — in every case — whether one does it oneself and depending only on oneself or whether one does it by asking someone to do it for one, the first condition: not to fear and to be calm. If you begin to boil and get fidgety in your body, it is finished, you can do nothing.

For everything — to live the spiritual life, heal sickness — for everything, one must be calm.[71]   THE MOTHER

Sweet Mother, when one sees an illness coming, how can one stop it?

Ah! First of all, you must not want it, and nothing in the body must want it. You must have a very strong will not to be ill. This is the first condition.

The second condition is to call the light, a light of equilibrium, a light of peace, quietude and balance, and to push it into all the cells of the body, enjoining them not to be afraid, because that again is another condition.

First, not to want to be ill, and then not to be afraid of illness. You must neither attract it nor tremble. You must not want illness at all. But you must not because of fear not want it; you must not be afraid; you must have a calm certitude and a complete trust in the power of the Grace to shelter you from everything, and then think of something else, not be concerned about this any longer. When you have done these two things, refusing the illness with all your will and infusing a confidence which completely eliminates the fear in the cells of the body, and then busying yourself with something else, not thinking any longer about the illness, forgetting that it exists... there, if you know how to do that, you may even be in contact with people who have contagious diseases, and yet you do not catch them. But you must know how to do this.

Many people say, "Oh, yes, here I am not afraid." They don't have any fear in the mind, their mind is not afraid, it is strong, it is not afraid; but the body trembles, and one doesn't know it, because it is in the cells of the body that the trembling goes on. It trembles with a terrible anxiety and this is what attracts the illness. It is there that you must put the force and the quietude of a perfect peace and an absolute trust in the Grace. And then, sometimes you are obliged to drive away with a similar force in your thought all suggestions that after all, the physical world is full of illnesses, and these are contagious, and because one was in contact with somebody who is ill, one is sure to catch it, and then, that the inner methods are not powerful enough to act on the physical, and all kinds of stupidities of which the air is full. These are collective suggestions which are passed on from one person to another by everybody. And if by chance there are two or three doctors, then it becomes terrible. (*Laughter*)[72]   THE MOTHER

There are minor methods [of stopping pain] and they have smaller results; they are not very easy either, that is, the knowl-edge of the power to cut the connection between the suffering part and the recording brain. One cuts the connection, then the brain does not register. That's what one does, what the doctors do with anaesthetics. They cut the connection of the nerves between the spot that's ill and the brain; so the brain no longer perceives anything or it is reduced to a minimum. And it always comes back to the same thing, one way or another; and all this calls for an occult power or a training. Some people have it spontaneously; there are not many of these — very few. But obviously, without going so far, there is one thing that one can try to do, it is not to concentrate on one's pain, to turn the attention away as much as possible, not think at all of one's pain, think as little as possible and above all not be concentrated on it, not to pay attention — "Oh, I'm in pain", then it becomes a little worse; "Oh, I'm in still greater pain", then it becomes still worse, like that, because one is concentrated on it; and this is the mistake one always makes: to think, be there, attentive, awaiting the sign of pain; then naturally it comes, it comes increased by the concentration of the attention given to it. That is why, when one is not well the best thing to do is to read or have something read, you see; it depends on the condition one is in. But if one can turn one's attention away, one no longer suffers.[73]   THE MOTHER

15

QUIET, CALM, PEACE, SILENCE

The quieter you are, the stronger you become. The firm basis
of all spiritual power is equanimity.[74]   THE MOTHER

Quiet is a condition in which there is no restlessness or disturbance.

Calm is a still unmoved condition which no disturbance
can affect — it is a less negative condition than quiet.

Peace is a still more positive condition; it carries with it
a sense of settled and harmonious rest and deliverance.

Silence is a state in which either there is no movement
of the mind or vital or else a great stillness which no surface
movement can pierce or alter.[75]   SRI AUROBINDO

Quietude is a very positive state; there is a positive peace which
is not the opposite of conflict — an active peace, contagious,
powerful, which controls and calms, which puts everything
in order, organises. It is of this I am speaking; when I tell
someone, "Be calm", I don't mean to say "Go and sleep, be
inert and passive, and don't do anything", far from it!... True
quietude is a very great force, a very great strength. In fact one
can say, looking at the problem from the other side, that all
those who are really strong, powerful, are always very calm.
It is only the weak who are agitated; as soon as one becomes
truly strong, one is peaceful, calm, quiet, and one has the

)wer of endurance to face the adverse waves which come
.shing from outside in the hope of disturbing one. This true
iietude is always a sign of force. Calmness belongs to the
rong.

And this is true even in the physical field. I don't know
? you have observed animals like lions, tigers, elephants, but
: is a fact that when they are not in action, they are always so
ierfectly still. A lion sitting and looking at you always seems
o be telling you, "Oh, how fidgety you are!" It looks at you
vith such a peaceful air of wisdom! And all its power, energy,
ihysical strength are there, gathered, collected, concentrated
ind — without a shadow of agitation — ready for action when
:he order is given.

I have seen people, many people, who could not sit still
for half an hour without fidgeting. They had to move a foot or
a leg, or an arm or their head; they had to stir restlessly all the
time, for they did not have the power or the strength to remain
quiet.

This capacity to remain still when one wants to, to gather
all one's energies and spend them as one wishes, completely
if one wants, or to apportion them as one wants in action,
with a perfect calm even in action — that is always the sign of
strength. It may be physical strength or vital strength or mental
strength. But if you are in the least agitated, you may be sure
there is a weakness somewhere; and if your restlessness is
integral, it is an integral weakness.[76]   THE MOTHER

... for the knowledge of the Self it is necessary to have the
power of a complete intellectual passivity, the power of dis-
missing all thought, the power of the mind to think not at all

which the Gita in one passage enjoins. This is a hard saying for the occidental mind to which thought is the highest thing and which will be apt to mistake the power of the mind not to think, its complete silence for the incapacity of thought. But this power of silence is a capacity and not an incapacity, a power and not a weakness. It is a profound and pregnant stillness. Only when the mind is thus entirely still, like clear, motionless and level water, in a perfect purity and peace of the whole being and the soul transcends thought, can the Self which exceeds and originates all activities and becomings, the Silence from which all words are born, the Absolute of which all relativities are partial reflections manifest itself in the pure essence of our being.[77]   SRI AUROBINDO

16

BODY

Body's Power of Self-Healing

Naturally, there are many ways of doing it [awakening in the body an aspiration for the Divine] and, in fact, each one should find his own. But the starting-point may be very different, apparently almost the very opposite.

In former times, when yoga was a flight from life, it was a common practice for people, apart from a few predestined ones, not to think about yoga until they were old, when they had experienced much, known all the vicissitudes of life, its pleasures, its sorrows, its joys and miseries, its responsibilities, disillusionments, indeed all that life usually brings to human beings; and naturally, all this had disabused them a little of their illusions about the joys of existence, so they were ready to think of something else, and their body, if not full of youthful enthusiasm (!), was at least not a hindrance, for as it had been satiated, it no longer asked for much.... To start from this end is all very well when one wants to leave life behind with a spiritual attitude and does not expect any collaboration from it in the transformation. This is obviously the easiest method. But it is also obvious that if one wants this material existence to *participate* in the divine life, to be the field of action and realisation, it is preferable not to wait until with wear and tear the body becomes sufficiently... quiet so as not to obstruct the yoga. It is much better, on the contrary, to take it quite young when it is full of all its energies and can put enough ardour and intensity into its aspiration. In this case, instead of relying on a weariness which no longer demands anything, one should rely on a kind of inner enthusiasm for the unknown, the new — for perfection. And if you have the good fortune to be in conditions where you can receive help and guidance from childhood, try while still very young to discern between the fugitive joys and superficial pleasures life can give and the marvellous thing that life, action, growth would be in a world of perfection and truth, where all the ordinary limitations, all the ordinary incapacities would be done away with.

When one is very young and as I say "well-born", that is, born with a conscious psychic being within, there is always, in the dreams of the child, a kind of aspiration, which for its child's consciousness is a sort of ambition, for something which would be beauty without ugliness, justice without injustice, goodness without limits, and a conscious, constant success, a perpetual miracle. One dreams of miracles when one is young, one wants all wickedness to disappear, everything to be always luminous, beautiful, happy, one likes stories which end happily. This is what one should rely on. When the body feels its miseries, its limitations, one must establish this dream in it — of a strength which would have no limit, a beauty which would have no ugliness, and of marvellous capacities: one dreams of being able to rise into the air, of being wherever it is necessary to be, of setting things right when they go wrong, of healing the sick; indeed, one has all sorts of dreams when one is very young.... Usually parents or teachers pass their time throwing cold water on it, telling you, "Oh! it's a dream, it is not a reality." They should do the very opposite! Children should be taught, "Yes, this is what you must try to realise and not only is it possible but it is *certain* if you come in contact with the part in you which is capable of doing this thing. This is what should guide your life, organise it, make you develop in the direction of the *true reality* which the ordinary world calls illusion."

This is what it should be, instead of making children ordinary, with that dull, vulgar common sense which becomes an inveterate habit and, when something is going well, immediately brings up in the being the idea: "Oh, that won't last!", when somebody is kind, the impression, "Oh, he will change!", when one is capable of doing something, "Oh, tomorrow I won't be able to do it so well." This is like an acid, a destructive acid in the being, which takes away hope, certitude, confidence in future possibilities.

When a child is full of enthusiasm, never throw cold water on it, never tell him, "You know, life is not like that!" You should always encourage him, tell him, "Yes, at present things are not always like that, they *seem* ugly, but behind this there is a beauty that is trying to realise itself. This is what you should love and draw towards you, this is what you should make the object of your dreams, of your ambitions."

And if you do this when you are very small, you have much less difficulty than if later on you have to undo, undo all the bad effects of a bad education, undo that kind of dull and vulgar common sense which means that you expect nothing good from life, which makes it insipid, boring, and contradicts all the hopes, all the so-called illusions of beauty. On the contrary, you must tell a child — or yourself if you are no longer quite a baby — "Everything in me that seems unreal, impossible, illusory, *that* is what is true, *that* is what I must cultivate." When you have these aspirations: "Oh, not to be always limited by some incapacity, all the time held back by some bad will!", you must cultivate within you this certitude that *that is* what is essentially true and *that is* what must be realised.

Then faith awakens in the cells of the body. And you will see that you find a response in your body itself. The body itself will feel that if its inner will helps, fortifies, directs, leads, well, all its limitations will gradually disappear.

And so, when the first experience comes, which some-times begins when one is very young, the first contact with the inner joy, the inner beauty, the inner light, the first contact with *that,* which suddenly makes you feel, "Oh! that is what I want," you must cultivate it, never forget it, hold it constantly before you, tell yourself, "I have felt it once, so I can feel it again. This has been real for me, even for the space of a second, and that is what I am going to revive in myself".... And encourage the body to seek it — to seek it, *with the confidence* that it carries that possibility within itself and that if it calls for it, it will come back, it will be realised again.

This is what should be done when one is young. This is what should be done every time one has the opportunity to recollect oneself, commune with oneself, seek oneself.

And then you will see. When one is normal, that is to say, unspoilt by bad teaching and bad example, when one is born and lives in a healthy and relatively balanced and normal environment, the body, spontaneously, without any need for one to intervene mentally or even vitally, has the certitude that even if something goes wrong it will be cured. The body carries within itself the certitude of cure, the cer-titude that the illness or disorder is sure to disappear. It is only through the false education from the environment that gradually the body is taught that there are incurable diseases, irreparable accidents, and that it can grow old, and all these stories which destroy its faith and trust. But normally, the body of a normal child — the body, I am not speaking of the thought — the body itself feels when something goes wrong that it will certainly be all right again. And if it is not like that, this means that it has already been perverted. It seems *normal* for it to be in good health, it seems quite abnormal to it if something goes wrong and it falls ill; and in its instinct, its spontaneous instinct, it is sure that everything will be all right. It is only the perversion of thought which destroys this; as one grows up the thought becomes more and more distorted, there is the whole collective suggestion, and so, little by little, the body loses its trust in itself, and naturally, losing its self-confidence, it also loses the spontaneous capacity of restoring its equilibrium when this has been disturbed.

But if when very young, from your earliest childhood, you have been taught all sorts of disappointing, depressing things — things that cause decomposition, I could say, disintegration — then this poor body does its best but it has been perverted, put out of order, and no longer has the sense of its inner strength, its inner force, its power to react.

If one takes care not to pervert it, the body carries within itself the certitude of victory. It is only the wrong use we make of thought and its influence on the body which robs it of this certitude of victory. So, the first thing to do is to cultivate this certitude instead of destroying it; and when it is there, no effort is needed to aspire, but simply a flowering, an unfolding of that inner certitude of victory.

The body carries within itself the sense of its divinity. There. This is what you must try to find again in yourself if you have lost it.

When a child tells you a beautiful dream in which he had many powers and all things were very beautiful, be very careful never to tell him, "Oh! life is not like that", for you are doing something wrong. You must on the contrary tell him, "Life *ought to be* like that, and *it will be* like that!"[78]

THE MOTHER

"Glorious Body" — Power of Transformation

Perfection is the true aim of all culture, the spiritual and psychic, the mental, the vital and it must be the aim of our physical culture also. If our seeking is for a total perfection of the being, the physical part of it cannot be left aside; for the body is the material basis, the body is the instrument which we have to use. Śarīram khalu dharmasādhanam, says the old Sanskrit adage, — the body is the means of fulfilment of dharma, and dharma means every ideal which we can propose to ourselves and the law of its working out and its action. A total perfection is the ultimate aim which we set before us, for our ideal is the Divine Life which we wish to create here, the life of the Spirit fulfilled on earth, life accomplishing its own spiritual transformation even here on earth in the conditions of the material universe. That cannot be unless the body too undergoes a transformation, unless its action and functioning attain to a supreme

> *capacity and the perfection which is possible to it or*
> *which can be made possible.*
>
> Sri Aurobindo, *The Supramental Manifestation*

Mother, how can the functioning of the body "attain
to a supreme capacity"?

Precisely by transformation. This implies a total transformation. Sri Aurobindo speaks about it later in what follows.

For the moment, our body is simply a doubtful improve-
ment on the animal body, for if we have gained from a certain
point of view, we have lost from another. It is certain that from
the point of view of purely physical capacities many animals
are superior to us. Unless by a special culture and transformation we succeed in really transforming our capacities, it could
be said that from the point of view of strength and muscular
power a tiger or a lion is far superior to us. From the point of
view of agility a monkey is far superior to us; and, for instance,
a bird can travel without needing any exterior mechanism or
plane, which is not yet possible for us... and so on. And we
are bound by the animal necessities of the functioning of our
organs; so long as we depend, for instance, on material food,
on absorbing matter in such a crude form, we shall be quite
inferior animals.

Therefore, I don't want to anticipate what we are going
to read, but all this purely animal functioning of our body, all
this part which is exactly the same as in animal life — that we
depend for life on the circulation of the blood and to have blood
we need to eat, and so on, and all that this implies — these are
terrible limitations and bondages! As long as material life
depends on that, it is obvious that we won't be able to divinise
our life.

So, we must assume that animality in the human being should be replaced by another source of life, and this is quite conceivable — not only conceivable but partially realisable; and this is obviously the aim we ought to set before ourselves if we want to transform matter and make it capable of expressing divine qualities.

In the very, very old traditions — there was a tradition more ancient than the Vedic and the Chaldean which must have been the source of both — in that ancient tradition there is already mention of a "glorious body" which would be plastic enough to be transformed at every moment by the deeper consciousness: it would express that consciousness, it would have no fixity of form. It mentioned luminosity: the constituent matter could become luminous at will. It mentioned a sort of possibility of weightlessness which would allow the body to move about in the air only by the action of will-power and by certain processes of control of the inner energy, and so on. Much has been said about these things.

I don't know if there ever were beings on earth who had partially realised this, but in a very small way there have been partial instances of one thing or another, examples which go to prove that it is possible. And following up this idea, one could go so far as to conceive of the replacement of material organs and their functioning as it now is, by centres of concentration of force and energy which would be receptive to the higher forces and which, by a kind of alchemy, would use them for the necessities of life and the body. We already speak of the different "centres" in the body — this knowledge is very widespread among people who have practised yoga — but these centres could be perfected to the point where they replace the different organs by a direct action of the higher energy and vibrations on matter. Those who have practised occultism well enough, in its most integral form, it could be said, know the process of materialisation of subtle energies and can put them in contact with physical vibrations. Not only is it something that can be done, but it is something which *is* done. And all that is a science, a science which must itself be perfected, completed, and which will obviously be used for the creation and setting in action of new bodies which will be able to manifest the supramental life in the material world.[79]

THE MOTHER

17

THE VITAL

On the physical plane the Divine expresses himself through beauty, on the mental plane through knowledge, on the vital plane through power and on the psychic plane through love.[80]

THE MOTHER

> *Will, Power, Force are the native substance of the Life-Energy, and herein lies the justification for the refusal of Life to acknowledge the supremacy of Knowledge and Love alone,—for its push towards the satisfaction of something far more unreflecting, headstrong and dangerous that can yet venture too in its own bold and ardent way towards the Divine and Absolute. Love and Wisdom are not the only aspects of the Divine, there is also its aspect of Power.*

Sri Aurobindo, The Synthesis of Yoga

... Sri Aurobindo says that the vital part, the vital being is the greatest obstacle because it is unregenerate, and that there would be a possibility of transforming it if it surrendered entirely to Love and Knowledge; but as its predominant quality is force, energy, power, it does not like to submit to other parts of the being, and this justifies its refusal to submit itself, for those virtues in their essence are as high as the others. That is why it has neither the same power nor the same capacities, for it is not developed, it has not surrendered, and this is what causes the dilemma: it does not submit because it has this power, and this power cannot be utilised...

If the vital were a mediocre being without definite qualities, there would be no difficulty in its surrendering, but it would be altogether useless. But, on the contrary, the vital is a sort of stronghold of energy and power — of all powers. Yet generally this power is diverted; it is no longer at the service of the Divine, it is at the service of the vital itself for its own satisfaction. So, as long as it is like that, it cannot be used.

It should come to understand that this energy and power which it feels within itself cannot become useful unless it enters into perfect harmony with the divine plan of realisation on earth. If it understands that, it becomes quiet and allows itself to be enlisted, so to say, in the totality of the being, and then it takes on its full strength and full importance. But otherwise, it cannot be used. And usually, all its activities are activities which always complicate things and take away their simplicity, their purity, often their beauty, and their effectiveness, for its action is blind, ignorant and very egoistic.[81]

THE MOTHER

Does depression come from the vital?

Oh, yes. All your troubles, depression, discouragement, disgust, fury, all, all come from the vital. It is that which turns love into hate, it is that which induces the spirit of vengeance, rancour, bad will, the urge to destroy and to harm. It is that which discourages you when things are difficult and not to its liking. And it has an extraordinary capacity for going on strike! When it is not satisfied, it hides in a corner and does not budge. And then you have no more energy, no more strength, you have no courage left. Your will is like... like a withering plant. All resentment, disgust, fury, all despair, grief, anger — all that comes from this gentleman. For it is energy in action.

Therefore, it depends on which side it turns. And I tell you, it has a very strong habit of going on strike. That is its most powerful weapon: "Ah! you are not doing what I want, well, I am not going to move, I shall sham dead." And it does that for the least reason. It has a very bad character; it is very touchy and it is very spiteful — yes, it is very ill-natured. For I believe it is very conscious of its power and it feels clearly that if it gives itself wholly, there is nothing that will resist the momentum of its force. And like all people who have a weight in the balance, the vital also bargains: "I shall give you my energy, but you must do what I want. If you do not give me what I ask for, well, I withdraw my energy." And you will be flat as a pancake. And it is true, it happens like that.

It is difficult to regulate it. Yet naturally, when you have succeeded in taming it, you have something powerful in hand for realisation. It is that which can carry by storm the biggest obstacles. It is that which is capable of turning an idiot into an intelligent person — it alone can do so; for if one yearns passionately for progress, if the vital takes it into its head that one must progress, even the greatest idiot can become intelligent! I have seen this, I am not speaking from hearsay; I have seen it, I have seen people who were dull, stupid, incapable of understanding, who understood nothing — you could go on explaining something to them for months, it would not enter, as though one were speaking to a block of wood — and then all of a sudden their vital was caught in a passion; they wanted simply to please someone or get something, and for that one had to understand, one had to know, it was necessary. Well, they set everything moving, they shook up the sleeping mind, they poured energy into all the corners where there was none; and they understood, they became intelligent. I knew someone who knew nothing practically, understood nothing, and who, when the mind started moving and the passion for progress took possession of him, began to write wonderful things. I have them with me. And when the movement withdrew, when the vital went on strike (for sometimes it went on strike, and withdrew), the person became once again absolutely dull.

Naturally it is very difficult to establish a constant contact between the most external physical consciousness and the psychic consciousness, and oh! the physical consciousness has plenty of goodwill; it is very regular, it tries a great deal, but it is slow and heavy, it takes long, it is difficult to move it. It does not get tired, but it makes no effort; it goes its way, quietly. It can take centuries to put the external consciousness in contact with the psychic. But for some reason or other the vital takes a hand in it. A passion seizes it. It wants this contact (for some reason or other, which is not always a spiritual reason), but it wants this contact. It wants it with all its energy, all its strength, all its passion, all its fervour: in three months the thing is done.

So then, take great care of it. Treat it with great consideration but never submit to it. For it will drag you into all kinds of troublesome and untoward experiments; and if you succeed in convincing it in some way or other, then you will advance with giant strides on the path.[82]   THE MOTHER

This rule of different selves in us is at the root of the stages of the development of human personality.... In some human beings it is the physical Purusha, the being of body, who dominates the mind, will and action; there is then created the physical man mainly occupied with his corporeal life and habitual needs, impulses, life-habits, mind-habits, body-habits, looking very little or not at all beyond that, subordinating and restricting all his other tendencies and possibilities to that narrow formation. But even in the physical man there are other elements and he cannot live altogether as the human animal concerned with birth and death and procreation and the satisfaction of common impulses and desires and the maintenance of the life and the body: this is his normal type of personality, but it is crossed, however feebly, with influences by which he can proceed, if they are developed, to a higher human evolution. If the inner subtle-physical Purusha insists, he can arrive at the idea of a finer, more beautiful and perfect physical life and hope or attempt to realise it in his own or in the collective or group existence. In others it is the vital self, the being of life, who dominates and rules the mind, the will, the action; then is created the vital man, concerned with self-affirmation, self-aggrandisement, life-enlargement, satisfaction of ambition and passion and impulse and desire, the claims of his ego, domination, power, excitement, battle and struggle, inner and outer adventure: all else is incidental or subordinated to this movement and building and expression of the vital ego. But still in the vital man too there are or can be other elements of a growing mental or spiritual character, even if these happen to be less developed than his life-personality and life-power. The nature of the vital man is more active, stronger and more mobile, more turbulent and chaotic, often to the point of being quite unregulated, than that of the physical man who holds on to the soil and has a certain material poise and balance, but it is more kinetic and creative: for the element of the vital being is not earth but air; it has more movement, less status. A vigorous vital mind and will can grasp and govern the kinetic vital energies, but it is more by a forceful compulsion and constraint than by a harmonisation of the being. If, however, a strong vital personality, mind and will can get the reasoning intelligence to give it a firm support and be its minister, then a certain kind of forceful formation can be made, more or less balanced but always powerful, successful and effective, which can impose itself on the nature and environment and arrive at a strong self-affirmation in life and action.[83]   SRI AUROBINDO

18

MIND

At a higher stage of the evolution of personality [above that of the vital self, the being of life] the being of mind may rule; there is then created the mental man who lives predominantly in the mind as the others live in the vital or the physical nature. The mental man tends to subordinate to his mental self-expression, mental aims, mental interests or to a mental idea or ideal the rest of his being: because of the difficulty of this subordination and its potent effect when achieved, it is at once more difficult for him and easier to arrive at a harmony of his nature. It is easier because the mental will once in control can convince by the power of the reasoning intelligence and at the same time dominate, compress or suppress the life and the body and their demands, arrange and harmonise them, force them to be its instruments, even reduce them to a minimum so that they shall not disturb the mental life or pull it down from its ideative or idealising movement. It is more difficult because life and body are the first powers and, if they are in the least strong, can impose themselves with an almost irresistible insistence on the mental ruler. Man is a mental being and the mind is the leader of his life and body; but this is a leader who is much led by his followers and has sometimes no other will than what they impose on him. Mind in spite of its power is often impotent before the inconscient and subconscient which obscure its clarity and carry it away on the tide of instinct or impulse; in spite of its clarity it is

fooled by vital and emotional suggestions into giving sanction
to ignorance and error, to wrong thought and to wrong action,
or it is obliged to look on while the nature follows what it
knows to be wrong, dangerous or evil. Even when it is strong
and clear and dominant, Mind, though it imposes a certain, a
considerable mentalised harmony, cannot integrate the whole
being and nature. These harmonisations by an inferior control
are, besides, inconclusive, because it is one part of the nature
which dominates and fulfils itself while the others are coerced
and denied their fullness. They can be steps on the way, but not
final; therefore in most men there is no such sole dominance
and effected partial harmony, but only a predominance and for
the rest an unstable equilibrium of a personality half formed,
half in formation, sometimes a disequilibrium or unbalance
due to the lack of a central government or the disturbance of a
formerly achieved partial poise. All must be transitional until
a first, though not a final, true harmonisation is achieved by
finding our real centre.[84]   SRI AUROBINDO

There are people — as soon as the least thing happens to their
body, their mind is completely upset. There are others still
who may be very ill and yet keep their mind clear. It is rarer
and more difficult to see a mind that's upset and the body
remaining healthy — it is not impossible but it is much rarer,
for the body depends a great deal on the state of the mind.
The mind (I have written it there in the book[1]) is the master
of the physical being. And I have said the latter was a very
docile and obedient servant. Only one doesn't know how to

---

[1] "The Science of Living", *On Education*

use one's mind, rather the opposite. Not only does one not know how to use it, but one uses it ill — as badly as possible. The mind has a considerable power of formation and a direct action on the body, and usually one uses this power to make oneself ill. For as soon as the least thing goes wrong, the mind begins to shape and build all the catastrophes possible, to ask itself whether it could be this, whether it could be that, if it is going to be like that, and how it will all end. Well, if instead of letting the mind do this disastrous work, one used the same capacity to make favourable formations — simply, for example, to give confidence to the body, to tell it that it is just a passing disturbance and that it is nothing, and if it enters a real state of receptivity, the disorder will disappear as easily as it has come, and one can cure oneself in a few seconds — if one knows how to do that, one gets wonderful results.[85]   THE MOTHER

Mind has a power also for truth; it opens its thought-chamber to Vidya as well as to Avidya, and if its starting-point is Ignorance, if its passage is through crooked ways of error, still its goal is always Knowledge: there is in it an impulse of truth-seeking, a power, — even though secondary and limited, — of truth-finding and truth-creation. Even if it is only images or representations or abstract expressions of truth that it can show us, still these are in their own manner truth-reflections or truth-formations, and the realities of which they are forms are present in their more concrete truth in some deeper depth or on some higher level of power of our consciousness.[86]

                                                  SRI AUROBINDO

A certain fundamental subjection of Mind to Life and Matter
and an acceptance of this subjection, an inability to make the
law of Mind directly dominant and modify by its powers the
blinder law and operations of these inferior forces of being,
remains even in the midst of our greatest mental mastery over
self and things; but this limitation is not insuperable. It is the
interest of occult knowledge that it shows us, — and a dynamic
force of spiritual knowledge brings us the same evidence,
— that this subjection of Mind to Matter, of the Spirit to a
lesser law of Life is not what it at first appears to be, a fundamental condition of things, an inviolable and unalterable rule
of Nature. The greatest, most momentous natural discovery
that man can make is this that Mind, and still more the force
of the Spirit, can in many tried and yet untried ways and in
all directions, — by its own nature and direct power and not
only by devices and contrivances such as the superior material
instrumentation discovered by physical Science, — overcome
and control Life and Matter.[87]   SRI AUROBINDO

Mind is a mediator divinity:
Its powers can undo all Nature's work:
Mind can suspend or change earth's concrete law.
Affranchised from earth-habit's drowsy seal
The leaden grip of Matter it can break;
Indifferent to the angry stare of Death,
It can immortalise a moment's work:
A simple fiat of its thinking force,
The casual pressure of its slight assent
Can liberate the Energy dumb and pent
Within its chambers of mysterious trance:

It makes the body's sleep a puissant arm,
Holds still the breath, the beatings of the heart,
While the unseen is found, the impossible done,
Communicates without means the unspoken thought;
It moves events by its bare silent will,
Acts at a distance without hands or feet.
This giant Ignorance, this dwarfish Life
It can illumine with a prophet sight,
Invoke the bacchic rapture, the Fury's goad,
In our body arouse the demon or the god,
Call in the Omniscient and Omnipotent,
Awake a forgotten Almightiness within.
In its own plane a shining emperor,
Even in this rigid realm, Mind can be king:[88]

SRI AUROBINDO

19

OCCULT POWERS OF THE SUBLIMINAL

Occultism means rightly the use of the higher powers of our nature, soul, mind, life-force and the faculties of the subtle physical consciousness to bring about results on their own or on the material plane by some pressure of their own secret law and its potentialities, for manifestation and result in human or earthly mind and life and body or in objects and events in the world of Matter. A discovery or an extension of these little known or yet undeveloped powers is now envisaged by some well-known thinkers as a next step to be taken by mankind in its immediate evolution....[89]

SRI AUROBINDO

Consciousness in its very nature could not be limited by the ordinary physical human-animal consciousness, it must have other ranges. Yogic or occult powers are no more supernatural or incredible than is supernatural or incredible the power to write a great poem or compose great music; few people can do it, as things are, — not even one in a million; for poetry and music come from the inner being and to write or to compose true and great things one has to have the passage clear between the outer mind and something in the inner being. That is why you got the poetic power as soon as you began yoga, — yogic force made the passage clear. It is the same with yogic consciousness and its powers; the thing is to get the passage clear, — for they are already within you. Of course, the first thing is to believe, aspire and, with the true urge within, make the endeavour.[90]   SRI AUROBINDO

The true and direct knowledge or vision of past, present and future begins with the opening of the psychical conscious-ness and the psychical faculties. The psychical consciousness is that of what is now often called the subliminal self, the subtle or dream self of Indian psychology, and its range of potential knowledge, almost infinite..., includes a very large power and many forms of insight into both the possibilities and the definite actualities of past, present and future. Its first faculty, that which most readily attracts attention, is its power of seeing by the psychical sense images of all things in time and space. As exercised by clairvoyants, mediums and others this is often, and indeed usually, a specialised faculty limited though often precise and accurate in action, and implies no development of the inner soul or the spiritual being or the higher intelligence. It is a door opened by chance or by an innate gift or by some kind of pressure between the waking and the subliminal mind and admitting only to the surface or the outskirts of the latter. All things in a certain power and action of the secret universal mind are represented by images, — not only visual but, if one may use the phrase, auditory and other images, — and a certain development of the subtle or psychical senses makes it possible, — if there is no interference of the constructing mind and its imaginations, if, that is to say, artificial or falsifying mental images do not intervene, if the psychical sense is free, sincere and passive, — to receive these representations or transcriptions with a perfect accuracy and not so much predict as see in its correct images the present beyond the range of the physical sense, the past and the future. The accuracy of this kind of seeing depends on its being confined to a statement of the thing seen and the attempt to infer, interpret or otherwise go beyond the visual knowledge may lead to much error unless there is at the same time a strong psychical intuition fine, subtle and pure or a high development of the luminous intuitive intelligence.

A completer opening of the psychical consciousness leads us far beyond this faculty of vision by images and admits us not indeed to a new time consciousness, but to many ways of the triple time knowledge. The subliminal or psychic self can bring back or project itself into past states of consciousness and experience and anticipate or even, though this is less common, strongly project itself into future states of consciousness and experience. It does this by a temporary entering into or identification of its being or its power of experiencing knowledge with either permanences or representations of the past and the future that are maintained in an eternal time consciousness behind our mentality or thrown up by the eternity of supermind into an indivisible continuity of time vision. Or it may receive the impress of these things and construct a transcriptive experience of them in the subtle ether of psychical being. Or it may call up the past from the subconscious memory where it is always latent and give it in itself a living form and a kind of renewed memorative existence, and equally it may call up from the depths of latency, where it is already shaped in the being, and similarly form to itself and experience the future. It may by a kind of psychical thought vision or soul intuition — not the same thing as the subtler and less concrete thought vision of the luminous intuitive intelligence — foresee or foreknow the

future or flash this soul intuition into the past that has gone
behind the veil and recover it for present knowledge. It can
develop a symbolic seeing which conveys the past and the
future through a vision of the powers and significances that
belong to supraphysical planes but are powerful for creation
in the material universe. It can feel the intention of the Divine,
the mind of the gods, all things and their signs and indices that
descend upon the soul and determine the complex movement
of forces. It can feel too the movement of forces that represent
or respond to the pressure — as it can perceive the presence
and the action — of the beings of the mental, vital and other
worlds who concern themselves with our lives. It can gather
on all hands all kinds of indications of happenings in past,
present and future time. It can receive before its sight the
etheric writing, *ākāśa-lipi*, that keeps the record of all things
past, transcribes all that is in process in the present, writes out
the future.

All these and a multitude of other powers are concealed
in our subliminal being and with the waking of the psychical
consciousness can be brought to the surface. The knowledge
of our past lives, — whether of past soul states or personal-
ities or scenes, occurrences, relations with others, — of the
past lives of others, of the past of the world, of the future,
of present things that are beyond the range of our physical
senses or the reach of any means of knowledge open to the
surface intelligence, the intuition and impressions not only
of physical things, but of the working of a past and present
and future mind and life and soul in ourselves and others,
the knowledge not only of this world but of other worlds or
planes of consciousness and their manifestations in time and
of their intervention and workings and effects on the earth

and its embodied souls and their destinies, lies open to our psychical being, because it is close to the intimations of the universal, not engrossed only or mainly with the immediate and not shut up into the narrow circle of the purely personal and physical experience.[91]   SRI AUROBINDO

The awakening of the psychical consciousness liberates in us the direct use of the mind as a sixth sense, and this power may be made constant and normal. The physical consciousness can only communicate with the minds of others or know the happenings of the world around us through external means and signs and indications, and it has beyond this limited action only a vague and haphazard use of the mind's more direct capacities, a poor range of occasional presentiments, intuitions and messages. Our minds are indeed constantly acting and acted upon by the minds of others through hidden currents of which we are not aware, but we have no knowledge or control of these agencies. The psychical consciousness, as it develops, makes us aware of the great mass of thoughts, feelings, suggestions, wills, impacts, influences of all kinds that we are receiving from others or sending to others or imbibing from and throwing into the general mind atmosphere around us. As it evolves in power, precision and clearness, we are able to trace these to their source or feel immediately their origin and transit to us and direct consciously and with an intelligent will our own messages. It becomes possible to be aware, more or less accurately and discerningly, of the activities of minds whether near to us physically or at a distance, to understand, feel or identify ourselves with their temperament, character, thoughts, feelings, reactions, whether by a psychic sense or a direct mental perception or by a very sensible and often intensely concrete reception of them, into our mind or on its recording surface. At the same time, we can consciously make at least the inner selves and, if they are sufficiently sensitive, the surface minds of others aware of our own inner mental or psychic self and plastic to its thoughts, suggestions, influences or even cast it or its active image in influence into their subjective, even into their vital and physical being to work there as a helping or moulding or dominating power and presence.[92]

                                                         SRI AUROBINDO

Sight, hearing, taste, smell, touch are really properties of the mind, not of the body; but the physical mind which we ordinarily use, limits itself to a translation into sense of so much of the outer impacts as it receives through the nervous system and the physical organs. But the inner Manas has also a subtle sight, hearing, power of contact of its own which is not dependent on the physical organs. And it has, moreover, a power not only of direct communication of mind with object, — leading even at a high pitch of action to a sense of the contents of an object within or beyond the physical range, — but direct communication also of mind with mind. Mind is able too to alter, modify, inhibit the incidence, values, intensities of sense impacts. These powers of the mind we do not ordinarily use or develop; they remain subliminal and emerge sometimes in an irregular and fitful action, more readily in some minds than in others, or come to the surface in abnormal states of the being. They are the basis of clairvoyance, clairaudience, transference of thought and impulse, telepathy, most of the more ordinary kinds of occult powers, — so called, though these are better described less mystically as powers of the now subliminal action of the Manas. The phenomena of hypnotism and many others depend upon the action of this subliminal sense-mind; not that it alone constitutes all the elements of the phenomena, but it is the first supporting means of intercourse, communication and response, though much of the actual operation belongs to an inner Buddhi. Mind physical, mind supraphysical, — we have and can use this double sense mentality.[93]

SRI AUROBINDO

There are powers of the mind and the life-force which have not been included in Nature's present systematisation of mind and life in matter, but are potential and can be brought to bear upon material things and happenings or even brought in and added to the present systematisation so as to enlarge the control of mind over our own life and body or to act on the minds, lives, bodies of others or on the movements of cosmic Forces. The modern admission of hypnotism is an example of such a discovery and systematised application, — though still narrow and limited, limited by its method and formula, — of occult powers which otherwise touch us only by a casual or a hidden action whose process is unknown to us or imperfectly caught by a few; for we are all the time undergoing a battery of suggestions, thought-suggestions, impulse-suggestions, will-suggestions, emotional and sensational suggestions, thought-waves, life-waves that come on us or into us from others or from the universal Energy, but act and produce their effects without our knowledge. A systematised endeavour to know these movements and their law and possibilities, to master and use the power or Nature-force behind them or to protect ourselves from them would fall within one province of occultism: but it would only be a small part even of that province; for wide and multiple are the possible fields, uses, processes of this vast range of little-explored Knowledge.[94]   SRI AUROBINDO

... in the phenomena of hypnosis not only can the hypnotised subject be successfully forbidden to feel the pain of a wound or puncture when in the abnormal state, but can be prevented with equal success from returning to his habitual reaction of suffering when he is awakened. The reason of this phenomenon is perfectly simple; it is because the hypnotiser suspends the habitual waking consciousness which is the slave of nervous habits and is able to appeal to the subliminal mental being in the depths, the inner mental being who is master, if he wills, of the nerves and the body. But this freedom which is effected by hypnosis abnormally, rapidly, without true possession, by an alien will, may equally be won normally, gradually, with true possession, by one's own will so as to effect partially or completely a victory of the mental being over the habitual nervous reactions of the body.[95]   SRI AUROBINDO

The power of occult seeing is there in everyone, mostly latent, often near the surface sometimes but much more rarely already on the surface. If one practises *trāṭak*, it is pretty certain to come out sooner or later, — though some have a difficulty and with them it takes time; those in whom it comes out at once have had all the time this power of occult vision near the surface and it emerges at the first direct pressure.[96]

SRI AUROBINDO

Subjective visions can be as real as objective sight — the only difference is that one is of real things in material space, while the others are of real things belonging to other planes down to the subtle physical; even symbolic visions are real in so far as they are symbols of realities. Even dreams can have a reality in the subtle domain. Visions are unreal only when these are merely imaginative mental formations, not representing anything that is true or was true or is going to be true.

This power of vision is sometimes inborn and habitual even without any effort of development, sometimes it wakes up of itself and becomes abundant or needs only a little practice to develop; it is not necessarily a sign of spiritual attainment, but usually when by practice of yoga one begins to go inside or live within, the power of subtle vision awakes to a greater or less extent; but this does not always happen easily, especially if one has been habituated to live much in the intellect or in an outward vital consciousness.[97]   SRI AUROBINDO

People value visions for one thing because they are one key (there are others) to contact with the other worlds or with the inner worlds and all that is there and these are regions of immense riches which far surpass the physical plane as it is at present. One enters into a larger freer self and a larger more plastic world; of course individual visions only give a contact, not an actual entrance, but the power of vision accompanied with the power of other subtle senses (hearing, touch, etc.) as it expands does give this entrance. These things have not the effect of a mere imagination (as a poet's or artist's, though that can be strong enough) but if fully followed out bring a constant growth of the being and the consciousness and its richness of experience and its scope.

People also value the power of vision for a greater reason than that: it can give a first contact with the Divine in his forms and powers; it can be the opening of a communion with the Divine, of the hearing of the Voice that guides, of the Presence as well as the Image in the heart, of many other things that bring what man seeks through religion or yoga.

Further, vision is of value because it is often a first key to inner planes of one's own being and one's own consciousness as distinguished from worlds or planes of the cosmic consciousness. Yoga-experience often begins with some opening of the third eye in the forehead (the centre of vision in the brows) or with some kind of beginning and extension of subtle seeing which may seem unimportant at first but is the vestibule to deeper experience. Even when it is not that, — for one can go to experience direct, — it can come in afterwards as a powerful aid to experience; it can be full of indications which help to self-knowledge or knowledge of things or knowledge of people; it can be veridical and lead to prevision, premonition and other openings of less importance but very useful to a yogi. In short, vision is a great instrument though not absolutely indispensable.

But, as I have suggested, there are visions and visions, just as there are dreams and dreams, and one has to develop discrimination and a sense of values and things and know how to understand and make use of these powers.[98]

SRI AUROBINDO

20

THE PSYCHIC

... the true central being is the soul, but this being stands back and in most human natures is only the secret witness or, one might say, a constitutional ruler who allows his ministers to rule for him, delegates to them his empire, silently assents to their decisions and only now and then puts in a word which they can at any moment override and act otherwise. But this is so long as the soul-personality put forward by the psychic entity is not yet sufficiently developed; when this is strong enough for the inner entity to impose itself through it, then the soul can come forward and control the nature. It is by the coming forward of this true monarch and his taking up of the reins of government that there can take place a real harmonisation of our being and our life.[99]   SRI AUROBINDO

Sweet Mother, is there a spiritual being in everybody?

That depends on what we call "being". If for "being" we substitute "presence", yes, there is a spiritual presence in everyone. If we call "being" an organised entity, fully conscious of itself, independent, and having the power of asserting itself and ruling the rest of the nature — no! The possibility of this independent and all-powerful being is in everybody, but the realisation is the result of long efforts which sometimes extend over many lives.

In everyone, even at the very beginning, this spiritual presence, this inner light is there.... In fact, it is everywhere. I have seen it many a time in certain animals. It is like a shining point which is the basis of a certain control and protection, something which, even in half-consciousness, makes possible a certain harmony with the rest of creation so that irreparable catastrophes may not be constant and general. Without this presence the disorder created by the violences and passions of the vital would be so great that at any moment they could bring about a general catastrophe, a sort of total destruction which would prevent the progress of Nature. That presence, that spiritual light — which could almost be called a spiritual consciousness — is within each being and all things, and because of it, in spite of all discordance, all passion, all violence, there is a minimum of general harmony which allows Nature's work to be accomplished.

And this presence becomes quite obvious in the human being, even the most rudimentary. Even in the most monstrous human being, in one who gives the impression of being an incarnation of a devil or a monster, there is something within exercising a sort of irresistible control — even in the worst, some things are impossible. And without this presence, if the being were controlled exclusively by the adverse forces, the forces of the vital, this impossibility would not exist.

Each time a wave of these monstrous adverse forces sweeps over the earth, one feels that nothing can ever stop the disorder and horror from spreading, and always, at a certain time, unexpectedly and inexplicably a control intervenes, and the wave is arrested, the catastrophe is not total. And this is because of the Presence, the supreme Presence, in matter.

But only in a few exceptional beings and after a long, very

long work of preparation extending over many, many lives does this Presence change into a conscious, independent, fully organised being, all-powerful master of his dwelling-place, conscious enough, powerful enough, to be able to control not only this dwelling but what surrounds it and in a field of radiation and action that is more and more extensive... and effective.[100] THE MOTHER

Has the psychic any power?

Power? It is usually the psychic which guides the being. One knows nothing about it because one is not conscious of it but usually it is that which guides the being. If one is very attentive, one becomes aware of it. But the majority of men haven't the least idea of it. For instance, when they have decided, in their outer ignorance, to do something, and instead of their being able to do it, all the circumstances are so organised that they do something else, they start shouting, storming, flying into a rage against fate, saying (that depends on what they believe, their beliefs) that Nature is wicked or their destiny baleful or God unjust, or... no matter what (it depends on what they believe). Whilst most of the time it is just the very circumstance which was most favourable for their inner development. And naturally, if you ask the psychic to help you to fashion a pleasant life for yourself, to earn money, have children who will be the pride of the family, etc., well, the psychic will not help you. But it will create for you all the circumstances necessary to awaken something in you so that the need of union with the Divine may be born in your consciousness. At times you have made fine plans, and if they had succeeded, you would have been more and more encrusted in your outer ignorance, your stupid little ambition and your aimless activity. Whilst if you receive a good shock, and the post you coveted is denied to you, the plan you made is shattered, and you find yourself completely thwarted, then, sometimes this opposition opens to you a door on something truer and deeper. And when you are a little awake and look back, if you are in the least sincere, you say: "Ah! it wasn't I who was right — it was Nature or the divine Grace or my psychic being who did it." It is the psychic being which organised that.[101]   THE MOTHER

The soul in itself contains all possible strength, but most of it is held behind the veil and it is what comes forward in the nature that makes the difference. In some people the psychic element is strong and in others weak; in some people the mind is the strongest part and governs, in others the vital is the strongest part and leads or drives. But by sadhana the psychic being can be more and more brought forward till it is dominant and governs the rest. If it were already governing, then the struggles and difficulties of the mind and vital would not at all be severe; for each man in the light of the psychic would see and feel the truth and more and more follow it.[102]

                                        SRI AUROBINDO

It seems to me impossible to escape from this necessity [of organising the being around the central Presence] if one wants to be and is to be a conscious instrument of the divine Force. You may be moved, pushed into action and used as *unconscious* instruments by the divine Force, if you have a minimum of goodwill and sincerity. But to become a conscious instrument, capable of identification and conscious, willed movements, you must have this inner organisation; otherwise you will always be running into a chaos somewhere, a confusion somewhere or an obscurity, an unconsciousness somewhere. And naturally your action, even though guided exclusively by the Divine, will not have the perfection of expression it has when one has acquired a conscious organisation around this divine Centre.

It is an assiduous task, which may be done at any time and under any circumstances, for you carry within yourself all the elements of the problem. You don't need anything from outside, no outer aid to do this work. But it requires great perseverance, a sort of tenacity, for very often it happens that there are bad "creases" in the being, habits — which come from all sorts of causes, which may come from atavistic malformation or also from education or from the environment you have lived in or from many other causes. And these bad creases you try to smooth out, but they wrinkle up again. And then you must begin the work over again, often, many, many, many a time, without getting discouraged, before the final result is obtained. But nothing and nobody can prevent you from doing it, nor any circumstance. For you carry within yourself the problem and the solution.[103]   THE MOTHER

21

INTUITION

Mother, how can the faculty of intuition be developed?

There are different kinds of intuition, and we carry these capacities within us. They are always active to some extent but we don't notice them because we don't pay enough attention to what is going on in us.

Behind the emotions, deep within the being, in a consciousness seated somewhere near the level of the solar plexus, there is a sort of prescience, a kind of capacity for foresight, but not in the form of ideas: rather in the form of feelings, almost a perception of sensations. For instance, when one is going to decide to do something, there is sometimes a kind of uneasiness or inner refusal, and usually, if one listens to this deeper indication, one realises that it was justified.

In other cases there is something that urges, indicates, insists — I am not speaking of impulses, you understand, of all the movements which come from the vital and much lower still — indications which are behind the feelings, which come from the affective part of the being; there too one can receive a fairly sure indication of the thing to be done. These are forms of intuition or of a higher instinct which can be cultivated by observation and also by studying the results. Naturally, it must be done very sincerely, objectively, without prejudice. If one wants to see things in a particular way and at the same time practise this observation, it is all useless. One must do it as if one were looking at what is happening from outside oneself, in someone else.

It is one form of intuition and perhaps the first one that usually manifests.

There is also another form but that one is much more difficult to observe because for those who are accustomed to think, to act by reason — not by impulse but by reason — to reflect before doing anything, there is an extremely swift process from cause to effect in the half-conscious thought which prevents you from seeing the line, the whole line of reasoning and so you don't think that it is a chain of reasoning, and that is quite deceptive. You have the impression of an intuition but it is not an intuition, it is an extremely rapid subconscious reasoning, which takes up a problem and goes straight to the conclusions. This must not be mistaken for intuition.

In the ordinary functioning of the brain, intuition is something which suddenly falls like a drop of light. If one has the faculty, the beginning of a faculty of mental vision, it gives the impression of something coming from outside or above, like a little impact of a drop of light in the brain, absolutely independent of all reasoning.

This is perceived more easily when one is able to silence one's mind, hold it still and attentive, arresting its usual functioning, as if the mind were changed into a kind of mirror turned towards a higher faculty in a sustained and silent attention. That too one can learn to do. One *must* learn to do it, it is a necessary discipline.

When you have a question to solve, whatever it may be, usually you concentrate your attention here (*pointing between the eyebrows*), at the centre just above the eyes, the centre of the conscious will. But then if you do that, you cannot be in contact with intuition. You can be in contact with the source of the will, of effort, even of a certain kind of knowledge, but in the outer, almost material field; whereas, if you want to contact the intuition, you must keep this (*Mother indicates the forehead*) completely immobile. Active thought must be stopped as far as possible and the entire mental faculty must form — at the top of the head and a little further above if possible — a kind of mirror, very quiet, very still, turned upwards, in silent, very concentrated attention. If you succeed, you can — perhaps not immediately — but you can have the perception of the drops of light falling upon the mirror from a still unknown region and expressing themselves as a conscious thought which has no connection with all the rest of your thought since you have been able to keep it silent. That is the real beginning of the intellectual intuition.

It is a discipline to be followed. For a long time one may try and not succeed, but as soon as one succeeds in making a "mirror", still and attentive, one always obtains a result, not necessarily with a precise form of thought but always with the sensations of a light coming from above. And then, if one can receive this light coming from above without entering immediately into a whirl of activity, receive it in calm and silence and let it penetrate deep into the being, then after a while it expresses itself either as a luminous thought or as a very precise indication here (*Mother indicates the heart*), in this other centre.

Naturally, first these two faculties must be developed; then, as soon as there is any result, one must observe the result, as I said, and see the connection with what is happening, the consequences: see, observe very attentively what has come in, what may have caused a distortion, what one has added by way of more or less conscious reasoning or the intervention of a lower will, also more or less conscious; and it is by a very deep study — indeed, almost of every moment, in any case daily and very frequent — that one succeeds in developing one's intuition. It takes a long time. It takes a long time and there are ambushes: one can deceive oneself, take for intuitions subconscious wills which try to manifest, indications given by impulses one has refused to receive openly, indeed all sorts of difficulties. One must be prepared for that. But if one persists, one is sure to succeed.

And there comes a time when one feels a kind of inner guidance, something which is leading one very perceptibly in all that one does. But then, for the guidance to have its maximum power, one must naturally add to it a conscious surrender: one must be sincerely determined to follow the indication given by the higher force. If one does that, then... one saves years of study, one can seize the result extremely rapidly. If one also does that, the result comes very rapidly. But for that, it must be done with sincerity and... a kind of inner spontaneity. If one wants to try without this surrender, one may succeed — as one can also succeed in developing one's personal will and making it into a very considerable power — but that takes a very long time and one meets many obstacles and the result is very precarious; one must be very persistent, obstinate, persevering, and one is sure to succeed, but only after a great labour.

Make your surrender with a sincere, complete self-giving, and you will go ahead at full speed, you will go much faster — but you must not do this calculatingly, for that spoils everything![104]   THE MOTHER

Intuition has a fourfold power. A power of revelatory truth-seeing, a power of inspiration or truth-hearing, a power of truth-touch or immediate seizing of significance, which is akin to the ordinary nature of its intervention in our mental intelligence, a power of true and automatic discrimination of the orderly and exact relation of truth to truth, — these are the fourfold potencies of Intuition. Intuition can therefore perform all the action of reason, — including the function of logical intelligence, which is to work out the right relation of things and the right relation of idea with idea, — but by its own superior process and with steps that do not fail or falter. It takes up also and transforms into its own substance not only the mind of thought, but the heart and life and the sense and physical consciousness: already all these have their own peculiar powers of intuition derivative from the hidden Light; the pure power descending from above can assume them all into itself and impart to these deeper heart-perceptions and life-perceptions and the divinations of the body a greater integrality and perfection. It can thus change the whole consciousness into the stuff of Intuition; for it brings its own greater radiant movement into the will, into the feelings and emotions, the life-impulses, the action of sense and sensation, the very workings of the body-consciousness; it recasts them in the light and power of truth and illumines their knowledge and their ignorance.[105]

SRI AUROBINDO

22

SPIRIT

What is the role of the spirit?

One might say that it is both the conscious intermediary between the Supreme and the manifestation, and the meeting-place of the manifestation with the Supreme.

Spirit is capable of understanding and communicating with the highest Godhead and at the same time it is the purest, one might say the least distorted intermediary of the highest Godhead in the outermost manifestation. It is spirit which, with the help of the soul, turns the consciousness towards the Highest, the Divine, and it is in the spirit that the consciousness can begin to understand the Divine.

It might be said that what is called "spirit" is the atmosphere brought into the material world by the Grace so that it may awaken to the consciousness of its origin and aspire to return to it. It is indeed a kind of atmosphere which liberates, opens the doors, sets the consciousness free. This is what enables the realisation of the truth and gives aspiration its full power of accomplishment.

From a higher standpoint, this could be put in another way: it is this action, this luminous and liberating influence that is known as "spirit". All that opens to us the road to the supreme realities, pulls us out from the mud of the Ignorance in which we are stuck, opens the doors to us, shows us the path, leads us to where we have to go — this is what man has called "spirit". It is the atmosphere created by the Divine

Grace in the universe to save it from the darkness into which it has fallen.

The soul is a kind of individual concentration of this Grace, its individual representative in the human being. The soul is something particular to humanity, it exists only in man. It is like a particular expression of the spirit in the human being. The beings of the other worlds do not have a soul, but they can live in the spirit. One might say that the soul is a delegation of the spirit in mankind, a special help to lead it faster. It is the soul that makes individual progress possible. The spirit, in its original form, has a more general, more collective action.

For the moment the spirit plays the part of a helper and guide, but it is not the all-powerful master of the material manifestation; when the Supermind is organised into a new world, the spirit will become the master and govern Nature in a clear and visible way.

What is called "new birth" is the birth into the spiritual life, the spiritual consciousness; it is to carry in oneself something of the spirit which, individually, through the soul, can begin to rule the life and be the master of existence. But in the supramental world, the spirit will be the master of this entire world and all its manifestations, all its expressions, consciously, spontaneously, naturally.

In the individual existence, that is what makes all the difference; so long as one just speaks of the spirit and it is something one has read about, whose existence one vaguely knows about, but not a very concrete reality for the consciousness, this means that one is not born into the spirit. And when one is born into the spirit, it becomes something much more concrete, much more living, much more real, much more tangible than the whole material world. And this is what makes the essential difference between beings. When *that* becomes spontaneously real — the true, concrete existence, the atmosphere one can freely breathe — then one knows one has crossed over to the other side. But so long as it is something rather vague and hazy — you have heard about it, you know that it exists, but... it has no concrete reality — well, this means that the new birth has not yet taken place. As long as you tell yourself, "Yes, this I can see, this I can touch, the pain I suffer from, the hunger that torments me, the sleep that makes me feel heavy, this is real, this is concrete... " (*Mother laughs*), that means that you have not yet crossed over to the other side, you are not born into the spirit.

(*Silence*)

In fact, the vast majority of men are like prisoners with all the doors and windows closed, so they suffocate, which is quite natural. But they have with them the key that opens the doors and windows, and they do not use it.... Certainly there is a time when they don't know they have the key, but long after they have come to know it, long after they have been told about it, they hesitate to use it and doubt whether it has the power to open the doors and windows or even that it is a good thing to open them! And even when they feel that "after all, it might be good", there remains some fear: "What will happen when these doors and windows are opened?... " and they are afraid. They are afraid of being lost in that light and freedom. They want to remain what they call "themselves". They like their falsehood and their bondage. Something in them likes it and goes on clinging to it. They still have the impression that without their limits they would no longer exist.

That is why the journey is so long, that is why it is difficult. For if one truly consented to cease to exist, everything would become so easy, so swift, so luminous, so joyful — but perhaps not in the way men understand joy and ease. In truth, there are very few people who do not enjoy fighting. There are very few who could accept the absence of night, few can conceive of light except as the opposite of darkness: "Without shadows there would be no picture. Without struggle, there would be no victory. Without suffering there would be no joy." That is what they think, and so long as one thinks in this way, one is not yet born into the spirit.[106]   THE MOTHER

Power of Spiritual Contagion

Sweet Mother, how can someone who hasn't much spiritual capacity best help in this work?

I don't know whether one can say that anyone has much or little spiritual capacity. It is not like that.

To live the spiritual life, a reversal of consciousness is needed. This cannot be compared in any way with the different faculties or possibilities one has in the mental field. It may be said of someone that he hasn't much mental, vital or physical capacity, that his possibilities are very limited; in that case it may be asked how these capacities may be developed, that is, how new ones may be acquired, which is something rather difficult. But to live the spiritual life is to open to another world within oneself. It is to reverse one's consciousness, as it were. The ordinary human consciousness, even in the most developed, even in men of great talent and great realisation, is a movement turned outwards — all the energies are directed outwards, the whole consciousness is spread outwards; and if anything is turned inwards, it is very little, very rare, very fragmentary, it happens only under the pressure of very special circumstances, violent shocks, the shocks life gives precisely with the intention of slightly reversing this movement of exteriorisation of the consciousness.

But all who have lived a spiritual life have had the same experience: all of a sudden something in their being has been reversed, so to speak, has been turned suddenly and sometimes completely inwards, and also at the same time upwards, from within upwards — but it is not an external "above", it is within, deep, something other than the heights as they are physically conceived. Something has literally been turned over. There has been a decisive experience and the standpoint in life, the way of looking at life, the attitude one takes in relation to it, has suddenly changed, and in some cases quite definitively, irrevocably.

And as soon as one is turned towards the spiritual life and reality, one touches the Infinite, the Eternal, and there can no longer be any question of a greater or smaller number of capacities or possibilities. It is the *mental* conception of spiritual life which may say that one has more or less capacity to live spiritually, but this is not at all an adequate statement. What may be said is that one is more or less ready for the decisive and total reversal. In reality, it is the mental capacity to withdraw from ordinary activities and to set out in search of the spiritual life which can be measured.

But so long as one is in the mental field, in this state, as it were, on this plane of consciousness, one can't do much

for others, either for life in general or for particular indi-
viduals, because one doesn't have the certitude oneself, one
doesn't have the definitive experience, the consciousness has
not been established in the spiritual world; and all that can be
said is that they are mental activities which have their good
and bad sides, but not much power and, in any case, not this
power of spiritual contagion which is the only truly effective
power.

The only thing that is truly effective is the possibility of
transferring to others the state of consciousness in which one
lives oneself. But this power cannot be invented. One cannot
imitate it, cannot seem to have it; it only comes spontaneously
when one is established in that state oneself, when one *lives*
within it and not when one is trying to live within it — when
one *is* there. And that is why all those who truly have a spiritual
life cannot be deceived.

An imitation of spiritual life may delude people who still
live in the mind, but those who have realised this reversal of
consciousness in themselves, whose relation with the outer
being is completely different, cannot be deceived and cannot
make a mistake.

It is these people the mental being does not understand.
So long as one is in the mental consciousness, even the highest,
and sees the spiritual life from outside, one judges with one's
mental faculties, with the habit of seeking, erring, correcting,
progressing, and seeking once again; and one thinks that those
who are in the spiritual life suffer from the same incapacity,
but that is a very gross mistake!

When the reversal of the being has taken place, all that
is finished. One no longer seeks, one sees. One no longer de-
duces, one knows. One no longer gropes, one walks straight to

the goal. And when one has gone farther — only a little farther — one knows, feels, lives the supreme truth that the Supreme Truth *alone* acts, the Supreme Lord *alone* wills, knows and does through human beings. How could there be any possibility of error there? What He does, He does because He wills to do it.

For our mistaken vision these are perhaps incomprehensible actions, but they have a meaning and an aim and lead where they ought to lead.

(Silence)

If one sincerely wants to help others and the world, the best thing one can do is to be oneself what one wants others to be — not only as an example, but because one becomes a centre of radiating power which, by the very fact that it exists, compels the rest of the world to transform itself.[107]   THE MOTHER

23

POWER SUPREME

The Guru [to the Student]:

Lift your eyes towards the Sun; He is there in that wonderful heart of life and light and splendour. Watch at night
the innumerable constellations glittering like so many solemn
watchfires of the Eternal in the limitless silence which is no
void but throbs with the presence of a single calm and tremendous existence; see there Orion with his sword and belt shining
as he shone to the Aryan fathers ten thousand years ago at
the beginning of the Aryan era; Sirius in his splendour, Lyra
sailing billions of miles away in the ocean of space. Remember
that these innumerable worlds, most of them mightier than our
own, are whirling with indescribable speed at the beck of that
Ancient of Days whither none but He knoweth, and yet that
they are a million times more ancient than your Himalaya,
more steady than the roots of your hills and shall so remain
until He at his will shakes them off like withered leaves from
the eternal tree of the Universe. Imagine the endlessness of
Time, realise the boundlessness of Space; and then remember
that when these worlds were not, He was, the Same as now,
and when these are not, He shall be, still the Same; perceive
that beyond Lyra He is and far away in Space where the stars
of the Southern Cross cannot be seen, still He is there. And
then come back to the Earth and realise who this He is. He
is quite near to you. See yonder old man who passes near
you crouching and bent, with his stick. Do you realise that

it is God who is passing? There a child runs laughing in the sunlight. Can you hear Him in that laughter? Nay, He is nearer still to you. He is in you, He is you. It is yourself that burns yonder millions of miles away in the infinite reaches of Space, that walks with confident steps on the tumbling billows of the ethereal sea; it is you who have set the stars in their places and woven the necklace of the suns not with hands but by that Yoga, that silent actionless impersonal Will which has set you here today listening to yourself in me. Look up, O child of the ancient Yoga, and be no longer a trembler and a doubter; fear not, doubt not, grieve not; for in your apparent body is One who can create and destroy worlds with a breath.[108]

SRI AUROBINDO

GLOSSARY

Adverse forces — forces opposed to spiritual progress or realisation.

ākāśa-lipi — the etheric writing.

Brahman — the Absolute; the Supreme Being; the One besides whom there is nothing else existent.

Buddhi — the thinking mind proper; the mental power of understanding; the discerning intelligence and enlightened will; the discriminating principle of mind, at once intelligence and will.

Chakras — centres of consciousness, seven in number, situated in the subtle body, each having a fixed psychological use and general function.

Gnosis — power beyond mind, based upon Truth of being; *see also* Supermind.

Gnostic — relating to Gnosis. *see* Gnosis.

Mahatma — a great soul; the term is used particularly by Theosophists to whom it means someone who has attained self-perfection and who acts as a guide for those who are still on the path.

Manas — mind, the mind proper [as distinct from the intellect (*buddhi*)]; sense-mind.

Mantra — sacred name, syllable or mystic formula

Mental, the — "mind" and "mental" connote specially that

part of the nature which has to do with cognition and intelligence, with ideas, with mental or thought perceptions, the reactions of thought to things, with the truly mental movements and formations, mental vision and will, etc. that are part of man's intelligence.

the Psychic — the soul; spark of the Divine before it has evolved into an individualised being; the divine essence in the individual. In the course of the evolution, the soul grows and evolves in the form of a soul-personality, the psychic being. The term is also often used for the soul-personality or the psychic being.

Purusha — Conscious Being; Conscious-Soul; a Consciousness behind that is the lord, witness, enjoyer, upholder and source of sanction for Nature's works; the Purusha represents the true being on whatever plane it manifests — physical, vital, mental, psychic.

the Subliminal — comprises the inner being, taken in its entirety of inner mind, inner life, inner physical, with the soul or psychic entity supporting them.

Supermind — the Supramental, the Truth-Consciousness, the Divine Gnosis, the highest divine consciousness and force operative in the universe. A principle of consciousness superior to mentality; it exists, acts and proceeds in the fundamental truth and unity of things and not like the mind in their appearances and phenomenal divisions.

Supramental — See Supermind.

Tratak — concentration of the vision on a single point or object.

the Vital — the Life-nature made up of desires, sensations,